The Beautiful People of the Book

A Tribute to Ethiopian Jews in Israel

by

Colette Berman and Yosef Miller

Jerusalem
1988

Dedicated to all the Ethiopian Jews now in Israel —

To those left behind, yearning for Zion —

And to the memory of those who perished on the way to Jerusalem.

Planning and Editing   *Colette Berman and Yosef Miller*

Photography Coordination
and Organization   *Colette Berman*

Text   *Yosef Miller*

Millhouse Publishers
P. O. Box 84259
Los Angeles, CA 90073
U.S.A.

Printed in Israel by Hamakor Press Ltd., Jerusalem
Graphic Design by Yvonne Fleitman

ACKNOWLEDGMENTS

Misgana ምስጋና

Most of the people listed below who helped make this book a reality know precisely that this word means "Thank you!" in Amharic. They have been long and deeply committed to the cause of Ethiopian Jews and we offer our sincerest appreciation to them for their help, advice, encouragement, and information which were invaluable in bringing the words and faces in this book to light.

Very special appreciation is extended to Mr. Menachem Begin for his monumental efforts on behalf of Ethiopian Jews and for having taken of his time to look over these photographs and sharing his reactions; and to his friend and secretary, Yehiel Kadishai, for his encouragement and help.

Warm personal thanks go to Professor Wolf Leslau of the University of California at Los Angeles and Professor Gideon Goldenberg of the Hebrew University in Jerusalem for their time, expert advice in Amharic usage, general knowledge, and calligraphy.

We also thank Rabbi Yosef Hadane, Shoshana Bendor, Dr. Jeff Halper, Dr. Steven Kaplan, Dr. Chaim Rosen, Dr. Michelle Schoenberger-Orgad, and other scholars and anthropologists in Israel who shared their knowledge and experiences with Beta Yisrael both in private and in the classroom and lecture halls.

We express our gratitude to Matityahou Atzmon, Zev Birger, David Brauner of the Jerusalem Post Photo Archives, Li Geipke, Uri Gordon, Effi Hellerstein, Shmuel Katz, Charlotte Leslau, Sonia Levitin, Sammy Mark, Uzi Peled, Benny Raphaely, Itzchak Pressburger, and Ronnie and Rosie Weisel. Special thanks are extended to Yossi Stern for kindly donating his art work; to Eric Ray for his calligraphy and art work; to Jack Roth for the innumerable hours he spent giving expert advice; to Shaare Zedek Medical Centre, Public Relations Department, Jerusalem, for their help with photographs; and to Israel Talby for his time and professional expertise.

We thank Leonard and Randy Kahn of Israel-American Baseball and the Netanya Little Leaguers who inspired everyone and who painfully talked to us of "home." Appreciation is also given to the American Association for Ethiopian Jews, The Center for Aid to Ethiopian Immigrants, the Jewish Agency, the Israel Ministry of Absorption, the National Council for Ethiopian Jews, The World Union of Jewish Students, and the Association for the Welfare of Soldiers in Israel.

A very warm note of appreciation is extended to Aida, the wife of Yosef Miller, for turning their home into an absorption center for an endless stream of Ethiopian immigrants and her word processor into the indispensable tool of this project.

We are most grateful to all our Ethiopian Jewish friends who came forward eagerly and lovingly to share their lives and experiences, their feelings, frustrations, worries, and hopes. Many of them are filled with their own tales of danger, courage, and adventure. It is because their stories are unfinished and their concern for loved ones ongoing that we are constrained in many instances not to use their full names.

First and foremost, we remember the insight and sensitivity of the late Yona Bogale who encouraged and advised us to his last days. Our warmest gratitudes goes out to: The artists Menachem Dunakau, Mulu Gete, and Daniel Meshesha; Mesfin Ambaw of the Association of Ethiopian Immigrants in Israel; Ferede A. and the seven-man National Rescue Committee; Assaf F., R.M., Tesfay A., David Z., and other activists for Family Reunification; Avraham N. of Ethiopian University Students; F. and his sisters and others who told us of the present dangers to their loved ones; and Brook and Aviva, Melkame and Birlie, Shmuel T., Rachel, and JJ—all of whom have become like members of our family.

We appreciate the *qesoch* who braved some tradition in acquiesing to photography, and shared their spirituality and wisdom. We also thank the brides and grooms who invited us to their joyous weddings, and the brave families in little flats who welcomed us grandly, poured out a profusion of talk, and often served *injera* and succulent *wat*. Most moving among them were the young women and mothers whose luminous faces grace these pages—working, studying, sometimes raising children in a one-parent family—all of them an inspiring part of *The Beautiful People of the Book*.

Colette Berman and Yosef Miller

MENACHEM BEGIN
Jerusalem

July 5, 1987.

Ms. Colette Berman
Rabbi Joseph Miller

Dear Ms. Berman and Rabbi Miller,

Thank you for your kindness in sending me the Album of our brethren, the Ethiopian repatriates. Looking at the pictures I said to myself in Hebrew:

יפים הם בני ישראל ובנותיו שבי ציון מאתיופיה

(Beautiful are the Bnei Israel who returned to our homeland from Ethiopia.) I pray that all our brethren will come to Israel and the families who were separated will be united.

With my best wishes to you and congratulations on the wonderful work you have done.

Yours sincerely,

M. Begin

The Ethiopian Jews — A Source of Inspiration

This book is the culmination of my desire to establish a permanent visual record—before their acculteration—of the warmth and sadness, pain and joy, dignity and strength that I saw in the faces and eyes of the Jews of Ethiopia in Israel.

It all began when I saw an article complete with pictures in the Spring 1985 issue of "Heartbeat," the quarterly journal of Shaare Zedek Medical Center in Jerusalem. It was about Ethiopian Jews recently arrived in Israel. Amongst the pictures was one of a mother holding a child on her lap. Her regal bearing and beauty struck me immediately and I have kept that picture with me every since. Imagine my joy when I recently met her and her family.

I was eager to learn more about the Jews of Ethiopia and so took a short course offered by the Rothberg School for Overseas Students at Hebrew University which greatly enlightened me. I then wished to share with others the excitement of the discoveries I was making and so was born the idea of a book of photographs which was later expanded to include explanatory text so that readers would not only see but could also learn and thus better understand.

It has been my good fortune to have made many personal friends amongst Ethiopian Jews and my life has been enriched by them. I have learned about their background, customs, and feelings. I admire greatly their strength of character in the face of adversity, their calm demeanor and dignity at all times, their gentleness which is always evident, and their deep spiritual nature. The warmth and love that radiates amongst families and friends is a joy to behold. I am most grateful to them for so graciously welcoming me into their hearts and their homes and allowing me to participate in their celebrations and gatherings.

There remains, however, amongst nearly all Ethiopians in Israel at present, a great sadness, longing, and concern for the 16,000 that are still in Ethiopia facing a very precarious future. May their fervent hopes and prayers soon be realized for a way *must* be found to reunite these families. Only then will happiness light up these beautiful faces once again.

Colette Berman
Jerusalem and Los Angeles

כל המקיים נפש אחת כאלו קיים עולם מלא

One who saves a single life is said to have saved an entire world.
Talmud Sanhedrin

7

Unless you call out, who will open the door?

Ethiopian Proverb

Ethiopians love words, stories, and proverbs. One of their proverbs says: "Where the heart overflows, it comes out through the mouth." This volume would amend this to "it comes out through the eyes," the eye of the discerning photographer and those of his subjects whose eyes are ubiquitous and overpowering herein.

We have our proverbs too. "Beauty is in the eye of the beholder," and if "A picture is worth a thousand words," this is a very heavy volume indeed.

Those who come to know the Ethiopians in Israel often stand with heart overflowing, seeing their courage as they face unfamiliar pressures in a modern, fast-paced land and feeling their anguish as they speak of their relatives left behind in perilous circumstances... and through it all remaining diffident and of graceful bearing, a rare elegance and a quiet charm hovering over them like a Presence, crowning them with an unworldly glow that makes us realize that in some cases— certainly in that of Ethiopian Jews—"Beauty is *not* skin deep." The deeper beauty that heightens their physical loveliness stems, in no small part, from generations of devotion to the Torah of Moses.

The Jews, who have long been known as "The People of the Book," actually have a library of 27 books. "The People of the Scroll" would be a more precise name for the keepers of the Torah, containing the first five of these books, painstakingly lettered onto a rolled parchment by a scribe. Only Beta Yisrael are "The People of the Book." Their Bible, the *Orit*, is actually in book form, also written by hand on parchment. This is consistent with their literal interpretation of scripture, which refers to the Torah as a *book* five times in Chapter 8 of Nehemiah, read on their Holy Day of Renewal of the Covenant. *"And Ezra opened the book in the sight of all the People."* (Nehemiah 8:5)

The spiritual beauty that we see everywhere in the Ethiopian Jews who have come to live in Israel has inspired the theme of this volume which views them as *The Beautiful People of the Book.*

Living by the Book, they sometimes understood Torah in ways different than the rest of world Judaism, the conventional ways we call "rabbinic Judaism" in this volume.

Living by the Book, they were iconoclasts in the mold of Abraham, destroying idols from the earliest incursions of the gods of Axum and, for all of their historical memory, resisting a missionizing church.

Living by the Book, they seem—even in our day—to have stepped directly out of its pages, a biblical people of shepherds and farmers in the tradition of Jacob and the brothers of Joseph.

And now they were filled with wonder as they came back to the very place where Abraham walked and dug a well and planted a tamarisk tree. The promised renewal of the biblical life seemed at hand.

Then their wonder turned to misgiving as they discovered that Abraham's Beersheba has sprouted trucks and buses out of asphalt streets, and tall buildings and loud noises... oh yes, and people too, but strange ones, the wrong color, the wrong clothes, the wrong foods... even in the synagogue they had it all wrong—not a drum or *qachel* in sight, not a melody that was familiar and hardly a word that could be understood. Their dismay and, finally, their renewed hope will also be reflected in the faces that await you.

A personal word. Unwanted in our birthplace (Ben Gurion's home town in Poland), my parents and I migrated to America. Remembering what it meant to be a displaced minority may later have led me to run imperilled Jews underground to Israel... to years of concern with minorities and people in difficult circumstances... and to these last five years of intensive, oft joyful, experiences with the Beta Yisrael—who, as you will see, are a welcoming, loving people. Perhaps you will recognize then, that this is a work of love, dealing with real people whose tenuous situation is cause for concern. Perhaps these images of *The Beautiful People of the Book* will inspire you to find out more about them and their incredible story, and how, in some way, you can help in this humanitarian challenge.

Rabbi Yosef Miller
Netanya, Israel

The Amharic letter above is a vowel carrier and is used here as a divider whenever new subject matter is introduced. It seems to symbolize walking and is intended to move you ahead... all the way to the bibliography, so that the end of the book will be a beginning for you.

The Hebrew and Ethiopian wisdoms heading the introductory pages to each section contain universal values of both cultures. These sayings from the rest of the Jewish world would have the elders of the Ethiopian Jewish community sounding a great Amen—had they heard them in their mountain isolation.

CONTENTS

Northwest Ethiopia

Hills and mountains, rivers and streams, and hundreds of villages comprise the ancestral home of Beta Yisrael, around and north of Lake Tana, through the Semien Mountains and into Tigre province.

( ) Indicates district or area
Provinces are indicated in capital letters

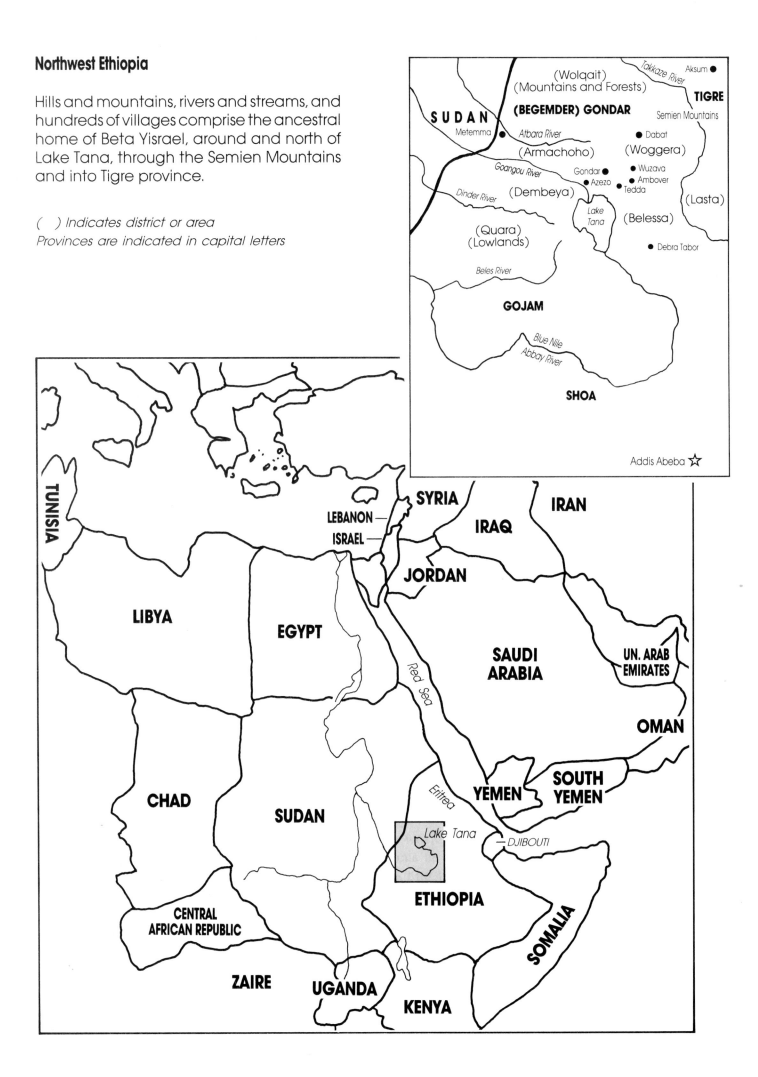

The Historical Setting

ታሪክ

tarik

If the survival of the Jewish people through two thousands years of exile and persecution is called a miracle, what word is there for the survival of that esoteric segment of it that calls itself *Beta Yisrael* (the "House of Israel") and by others was called *Falasha* ("stranger")?

No one can explain it. All we can do is contemplate the people in wonder and admiration and say: "But here they are!" Their long story, told briefly in these pages, will convince you that it is more than a wonder that the faces you are looking at belong to Ethiopian Jews who are alive and well and living in Israel. The faces themselves will elicit your admiration. You will find yourself turning the pages backwards as often as forwards to look at them again and again. They will make you glad they are still around to be photographed and seen. They almost weren't.

Some say there were over half a million Beta Yisrael at one time. There were apparently 150,000 to 200,000 a century ago. Faitlovitch, their friend and teacher, put their number in 1906 at only 50,000, and there are about 32,000 left today. Things move faster in the modern world... even in the wrong direction.

The Beta Yisrael (or *kayla*, as their enemies call them in an old Agau dialect) may soon have been snuffed out altogether, were it not for the existence of the State of Israel, which finally granted them full rights and status under its Law of Return, stating that "Every Jew has a right to immigrate to the country."

Amazing as was Jewish survival, we at least have a good idea of how it came to pass that an ancient people held on to the same book, language, laws, and dream of a return for twenty centuries in exile. The Children of Israel busied themselves with recording all their experiences in histories, and religious and secular literature of all kinds. The Beta Yisrael wrote and edited a number of unusual religious books, but they dealt mostly with a higher world and how to live a good life in this one in order to reach it. They wrote little, or nothing that has been preserved, about themselves.

As difficult as explaining their survival, is the question of how Jews came to exist in Ethiopia in the first place. Again, the Children of Israel answered the question of how they came to be from the beginning. In the first book of the Bible, we are taken carefully from the creation of the first man, to the vision of Abraham, the revelation at Sinai and the conquest of the Land. There, kings, prophets, and rabbis continued the shaping of the Jewish People.

All we can say of Beta Yisrael is that they were in Ethiopia from time immemorial. This admittedly is an overused phrase, but as it means that no one remembers, it has never been more aptly used than concerning the origins of Black Jews in Abyssinia, the older name for Ethiopia, or Cush, as Ethiopia is called in the Bible. Though a few scholars have doubts, most agree that there is substantial evidence for placing Jews in Abyssinia from a very early period—for example the clear influence of biblical ideas and symbols and the use of cognate Jewish Aramaic words in the Ethiopian translation of the Bible. The striking point here is that such Jewish influence existed in Ethiopia long before Christianity came to the country in the fourth century. When the Church took over in Ethiopia, it thus found many Jewish practices among the tribes, not eating animals forbidden by the Torah of Moses, observing the Sabbath on the seventh day of the week, and circumcision on the eighth day after birth.

All that goes to the question of when but says nothing about where, specifically, the Beta Yisrael came from. That, we have ultimately to answer the same way—from places immemorial. Clearly, though, they came from nearby countries, and though the evidence is largely circumstantial, it is sufficient to show that they came from three places at least, and in a sense, from four. Indications point to wanderings from Egypt, Yemen, Southern Arabia and, as the Beta Yisrael themselves believe, from Israel. The fourth, Ethiopia itself, would seem to require least proving, as racial characteristics and places of settlement confirm.

Eldad Hadani ("of the Tribe of Dan," as he calls himself in his highly imaginative style), writes in the 9th Century that in his travels he encountered a Jewish tribe "by the rivers of Cush." His story, the earliest record of Jews in Ethiopia, outlines the belief—based on the Bible and his own fancy—that the Beta Yisrael came from the Land of Israel itself. Solomon's Kingdom was split between Rehoboam, his son, and Jeroboam, who became King of Israel in the North. The Tribe of Dan, living in the furthest North, refuses to fight against its brothers in Judea and support a king not of the Davidic line. They may also have been offended by the Golden Calf Jeroboam set up in Dan (Kings I, 12:29).

They left Israel, eventually reaching Abyssinia, there to find others of the Ten Lost Tribes—Naftali, Gad, and Asher, and "they multiplied greatly and assumed power and wealth," Eldad tells us. This would date the first arrivals in Abyssinia to the 10th Century BCE.

Egypt figures prominently as the origin of Beta Yisrael in at least two separate periods—the first going back to the 6th Century BCE. The writings of Jeremiah (44:1) establish Elephantine as a site of Jewish settlement. It lies near Aswan of today on the upper Nile River and Hebrew soldiers were sent there to guard the southern Egyptian border not far from Ethiopia. Corroboration and information about the Jewish community there comes from the Elephantine papyri discovered only in our century. They had a temple of their own and brought sacrifices. Much later, in the 2nd Century BCE, we find the High Priest Onias building a Temple at Leontopolis and offering sacrifices there. He hoped with the Temple to unite quarreling groups. If these two groups from Egypt (separated by 400 years) found their way to Ethiopia, it would account for the practice of the Beta Yisrael in maintaining altars and sacrifices from the earliest times.

From beyond the rivers of Ethiopia, shall my suppliants,
my dispersed ones bring my offering.
The Prophet Zephaniah 3:10

Further support of Egyptian origin: The Bible of Beta Yisrael, written in ancient Ge'ez, has divergencies from the Hebrew Bible, suggesting that it had not been translated from the Hebrew. Comparisons show that the Ethiopic bible had been translated from the Septuagint, the Greek translation of the Hebrew Bible, and that could well have been brought to Ethiopia by Jews who came from Egypt where the Hellenistic influence was strong.

Pressures forced the earlier and later communities to move. Ptolemaic wars could have pushed the Elephantine community to follow the Nile to its source at Lake Tana, the area of Beta Yisrael settlement.

There is a problem with this supposed overland migration. Such a trek would prove very difficult, even allowing for the Blue Nile circling right up and into Ethiopia. "Up" is the key difficulty. There is quite a barrier at the mountain mass that crowns the Great Syrian Rift. The image of all of Ethiopia as a dry and parched desert came across strongly during the time of drought and starvation in 1984. In actuality, Ethiopia is a stunning country of mountains and rivers, forests, huge coffee plantations, the Blue Nile Falls and the remains of awesome volcanoes. *The Last of Days* (Farhi, see bibliography) will give you a powerful sense of all this. In the novel, a boat rushing down the terrifying, white water, rock-tossing river, calls up the image of the mythical Sambatyon—the stormy river that rests on the Sabbath—beyond which dwell the Ten Lost Tribes or (writes Eldad Hadani) the Children of Moses.

The view that Jews came from Yemen to Ethiopia is easier to support. Firstly, the countries lie quite close to each other on both sides of the Red Sea where trading vessels sailed with the winds from Solomon's times and before. Then, some of the skills of the Beta Yisrael may well have been learned from Yemenite Jews. Thirdly, the similarity of character and behavior traits of gentility and refinement remain striking to this day. Bolstering the Yemen theory is the fact that the Kingdom of Saba colonized Ethiopia for gold mining. Their obelisks still stand at Aksum which became the ancient capital of Abyssinia. They spoke *Ge'ez*, the Beta Yisrael language of scripture and prayer. Connections will become clearer if it is remembered that the biblical name of the region was Sheba (also called Saba), later called Himyar, which included Yemen of today.

The movement to Ethiopia was a long process. When a Yemenite king ruled Ethiopia, Yemenite Jews migrated freely to Ethiopia; and when the Ethiopian King Kaleb conquered Yemen, *circa* 525, Jews were forcibly brought to Ethiopia. Significant and surprising is the fact that the ruler whom King Kaleb of Aksum defeated was a Jewish King, Dhu Nhwas, ruler of Himyar.

The Jews of South West Arabia reached high influence in the 5th and 6th Centuries. They converted many pagan Arab tribes to Judaism. Since the connections between the Ethiopian Kingdom at Aksum and this region of Arabia were many, it is conceivable that the Jews of Arabia also influenced and converted the Ethiopians, or, again, that some migrated and remained.

Thus the immigration of Jewish peoples from nearby countries into Ethiopia went on for about a thousand years. The newcomers mixed with the local population, converted many of them and married them. They adopted their languages—Ge'ez, or old Ethiopic, for sacred texts, and the old Cushite languages for daily use. These were replaced by the national language, Amharic, for the Jews around Lake Tana, while those further north spoke Tigrinya. Through it all they held on to their Jewish ways. All was mixed and synthesized into what became the Beta Yisrael.

If the immigrants had hoped to escape from the upheavals in ancient Israel, Egypt, and Arabia to a tranquil, pastoral life they were to be sorely disappointed —though there were long peaceful periods. Due in great measure to the takeover of "their" country by the word and sword of Christianity, their history was anything but peaceful. There may have been an inherent restlessness as well in the transplanted "House of Israel"—something of the memories of intrigues and battles left behind.

Over and over, they found themselves in small wars, marching behind captains and kings, making and switching alliances, at the vortex of stormy struggles between faiths and kings, kingdoms and dynasties rising and falling, until, at the end of the road, the Beta Yisrael were all but extinct and all dynasties replaced by a "People's Revolution" which itself is beleaguered from all sides.

As you read the details of this history, well-told in several of the books listed in the bibliography, ask yourself how they held on to the Torah through all this, to their dream of angels and Isaiah's vision of universal peace...

> *And the wolf shall dwell with the lamb;*
> *And the leopard shall lie down with the kid;*
> *And the calf and the young lion and the fatling together;*
> *And a little child shall lead them.*

Isaiah 11:6

Perhaps it was Isaiah's promise, in the same prophecy, of the ingathering of the far-flung exiles of Israel, specifically naming them...

> *And it shall come to pass in that day,*
> *That the Lord will set His hand again the second time*
> *To recover the remnant of His people.*
> *That shall remain from Assyria, and from Egypt,*
> *And from Pathros, and from Cush...*

Isaiah 11:11

The troubles of the Jews had begun when the rulers of the Menelik dynasty at Aksum adopted Christianity in the fourth century. Perhaps it was then that they retreated to the mountain region around Lake Tana. No one has unearthed, as yet, any records telling the history of the next six centuries. There were only the tall tales of Eldad and those of the legendary Prester John, saintly and all-powerful Christian King of Ethiopia, who wrote frequently about his Jewish subjects (often in Hebrew).

There may have been some intervals of peace. We know only that the Jews never abandoned their heritage, though we can surmise a good deal of cajoling and pressure combined with military threats and incursions into the Beta Yisrael enclave by the forces from Aksum. By then, the centuries could have solidified the people, and those who strike roots in mountain areas are not easily driven off. The Beta Yisrael on the Simien heights clearly never developed the ghetto mentality of their brothers in most communities of the world during the Dark Ages.

The story now comes into sharper focus as the Abyssinian Royal Chronicles tell of the growth and strength of the Jews and their victories in battle. Islam was also on the march and Aksum was vulnerable. Around the year 950, the Beta Yisrael joined the Agau tribes, amongst whom they lived, in a full-scale rebellion against Aksum and Christianity. The Chronicles reports that it was Falasha Queen Judith (*Gudit*) who led the revolt. Stories proliferate about her origin and prowess, but the Beta Yisrael insist she was a Jewess named Esther. She apparently set

16

herself no less a task than the complete eradication of Christianity from the land. She destroyed Aksum, burned churches and monasteries and slaughtered priests and monks. Descriptions of such savagery were later reported in the Royal Chronicles and they succeeded in their goal of instilling a hatred and fear of the Jews that has hardly abated. A new dynasty came to power, the Zagwe (named for a supposed son of Solomon). There were eleven kings, five of them reportedly Jewish, who ruled during this Golden Age of the Beta Yisrael.

When the Menelik leaders resumed power, wars of retribution followed. It proved no easy task to defeat the Falashas (their name is so recorded in the Chronicles) and their allies. Emperor Amda Siyon defeated a new Falasha uprising in the 15th Century. Negus (king) Yshak had to fight the Falashas again in the 15th Century. Negus Za'ra Ya'kob, their greatest foe, fought them again so fiercely that he earned the title "Exterminator of the Jews." Note the Biblical names of the Christian rulers. The irony of it—"King Ya'kob, the Exterminator of the Jews." But his victories didn't end the matter. His son—said to have been born of his captive Jewish wife—was taught by the first Jewish monk, Abba Sabra, and himself became a spiritual leader of the Jews called Abba Tzaga.

None of the wars are conclusive, however, as the Muslims come again and again to join the battle against the Christians. We reach the 16th Century and there is a Falasha King, Yoram, who is killed and replaced by King Radai. He restores Falasha independence and gives Biblical names to the mountains of his kingdom. Now Negus Sarsa-Dengel launches the cruelest war against the Falashas. The Portuguese had brought cannon into the country and they prove decisive. The final battles of the Falashas are recorded in detail in the Chronicles and contain so many tales of heroism (bound to her captor, a Falasha woman hurls herself into a steep gorge, taking her oppressor down with her) that even the Chronicles were moved to compare them to the struggle on Massada against the Roman Legions.

There was yet another uprising. A leader named Gideon (following several other military leaders who assumed the name of the biblical hero) led the last Falasha resistance. He was defeated by King Susneyos, whom the Portuguese armed heavily, as he had converted to Catholicism. King Fasilidas, who ruled from 1632 to 1667 drove out the Portuguese and reestablished the Ethiopian Coptic clergy. It was he who built the castles at Gondar, but with Falasha hands as masons and ironworkers—unfortunate, as we shall see anon, for glowing iron in fire was looked upon as evil magic. Looking like misplaced Tudor castles, Fasilidas' towers stand to this day, "a wondrous mystery to behold," in the words of the Ethiopian Airlines poster.

We have here a chronicle of battles and heroism that would have astounded the Jews in the ghettos of Europe under the yoke of the Czars and the rack of the Inquisition. From Bar Kochba's last stand against the Romans (135 C.E.) to the Warsaw Ghetto uprising in 1943 and Israel's War of Independence in 1948, there was thought to be only submission and martyrdom in the diaspora.

Around the year 1000, when Shapiro of the German town of Speyer hid in a cellar with his family, hoping to protect it from the raging townsfolk who were coming once again to burn and pillage and possibly murder, he knew nothing of Queen Judith who ruled in Abyssinia, a powerful monarch controlling vast stretches of mountains and riverland that could have sheltered him and his family and all the frightened Jews of the Rhineland. Would he have fled to her had he known she was Jewish and her priests followed the ways of his Torah? If he could thus have saved the life of his daughter, also named Judith, why not!

17

But they knew nothing of each other... and independently they survived... or died. A Jewish kingdom, even a small one high in the Simien mountains, could have saved at least a million Jewish children from Hitler's "Final Solution." It might well have saved tens of thousands of Beta Yisrael who were killed by dervish invaders or died of starvation and plague in the last decades of the 19th Century. Still, Isaiah's remnant, from Europe and Africa, were about to be redeemed.

That they are in Israel at all, is due to the incredible Beta Yisrael themselves and to others of compassion who believe in justice and the freedom of man. It is also due to the G-d of history and some of His curious creatures like Eldad Hadani and Benjamin of Tudela, merchant and travelling adventurer who described the mountain Jews and caught the imagination of the world with the very possibility of the actual existence of the Beta Yisrael.

Based on Eldad's descriptions of the Lost Tribe of Dan and biblical references to "His People" in Cush, Chief Rabbi David ibn Zimra ruled in 16th century Cairo that those "from the Land of Cush are without doubt of the Tribe of Dan of the seed of Israel." This eventually led to the ruling in 1973 by the Sephardi Chief Rabbi of Israel, Ovadia Yosef, confirming the same and praying for the fulfillment of the prophecy of Isaiah (11:11) that *"the Lord... shall recover the remnant of His people."*

The prayer was answered in the miraculous days of the winter of 1984-5 with the new Exodus from Cush to Israel, when night after night, planeloads of Beta Yisrael flew into Ben Gurion airport, were bussed southward to a seaside resort and found themselves on the morrow—hundreds of men and women, mostly young with many children and suckling babies—scattered over a soft, green lawn, their white flowing gowns reflecting the Israeli sun, and the light of the African sun still shining from their feverish eyes and beautiful faces.

They were home!

Scholars must love the Falasha story. There is enough uncertainty, unclarity, contradiction and even mystery in it for endless speculations. Anthropologists, linguists, ethnomusicologists, professors of comparative religion, biblical critics and others continue to investigate the origins and the paths taken by the Beta Yisrael.

We have the writings of modern investigators, going back to the 18th Century who spent time in the villages around Lake Tana and the Simien Mountains with the Jews in the province of Gondar (formerly Begemder) and with those who established themselves more recently in the province of Tigre. These observers, it will be noted, were variously motivated.

James Bruce, famed Scottish explorer, spent two years in Gondar (1769-70) and brought back a large collection of Ethiopian manuscripts and much information about the life of the Falashas.

Antoine d'Abbadie, lived 11 years in Abyssinia from 1837 and published his impressions of the Falashas.

Filosseno Luzzatto, son of the great rabbinic scholar, Shmuel David Luzzatto, was caught up by the drama of the Falashas as told by Bruce and d'Abbadie and began writing and acting on behalf of the oppressed people. With solid Jewish grounding and with obvious passion for the recognition and rescue of these, his exotic brothers, Filosseno would certainly have moved up by half a century Jewish efforts to contact and "Save the Falashas" (a slogan that blossomed only in the

20th Century) had he not died in 1854 at the age of twenty-five, and without visiting those he wrote about.

Henry Aaron Stern, born a German Jew, came to Ethiopia in 1860, also to "save" the Falashas; but as convert and committed missionary, he promised Emperor Theodore of Ethiopia that he would "save" them for the Ethiopian Coptic Church. He did not win the Emperor's favor and was severly punished. His writings shed little light on the Jewish ways of the Falashas, but in recounting his exploits, he revealed the pressures to which they were subjected by the missionaries, paving the way for the next effort to ameliorate their lot.

As if to make up for F. Luzzatto's brief life, Joseph Halévi reached the age of ninety. Living in France, the Hebrew and Semitic scholar was chosen by the Alliance Israélite Universelle to visit the Jews in Abyssinia. This made him the first emissary sent by a Jewish organization to the Beta Yisrael. On and off, a living contact with the Jews of the world was maintained to the climactic time of Operation Moses and beyond.

Halévi's report in French and in an enlarged English version, Travels in Abyssinia, London, 1877, tells of his adventurous year, trying to reach the Falasha villages by following the British forces of General Robert Napier who invaded Ethiopia to free British captives (among them, Henry Stern). Halévi finally made his own way into the villages, where he remained a year. He tells how the Jews, suspicious of his motives, would not touch or welcome him. An inspiration, so brilliant it must have been sincere, came to Halévi and he said:
"I am, like you, an Israelite... *I also am a Falasha...* and acknowledge the law of Sinai!"
"What! You a Falasha! A white Falasha! You are laughing at us! Are there any white Falashas?"
(How could they know how often the Jew has been called stranger, invader, outcast... i.e., Falasha?)
I assured them that all the Falashas of Jerusalem, and in other parts of the world were white... The name of Jerusalem, which I had accidentally mentioned, changed as if by magic the attitude of the most incredulous.
"Have you beheld with your own eyes Mount Zion, and the House of the L-rd of Israel, the holy Temple?"

It took many years till the line of activists on behalf of Beta Yisrael began again, this time with a man who was to devote a lifetime to the education and succor of the Falashas. Jacques Faitlovitch, a student of Halévi, replaced his aging teacher as the next emissary to the ancient community of Jews in the mountains of northwest Ethiopia. Faitlovitch, more than any other person, brought the Falashas to the attention of the Jewish world and the teaching of normative Judaism to the Falashas. He set the wheels of redemption in motion, and he knew that they would not stop till the new Exodus was completed.

A rabbinic student from Lodz, Poland, Yankel Faitlovitch found his way to the Ecole des Hautes Études in Paris. In 1904 he set out for Ethiopia. It was the year in which a handful of his Polish contemporaries turned their faces toward Zion. The group—which included David Ben Gurion—would be the builders of the nation that would one day welcome the black Jews of Abyssinia. It was Faitlovitch's life of devotion to a cause that gave reality to an ancient hope. His life was a story of faith and action—finding, teaching and training young Beta Yisrael to teach and to assume leadership, from the devoted Getye Yermias and the brilliant Taamrat Emmanuel to Yona Bogale who would assume the mantle of leader, continue to establish schools, and strengthen the contact with the Jews of the world and the emigration to Zion.

Faitlovitch had to struggle against the limitations of World War II, hostile elements in Ethiopia and the changing governments. He made prodigious efforts to influence Haile Selassie to better the lot of the Beta Yisrael.

He also had a struggle with the Beta Yisrael, to accept and trust him, and to accept other and "strange" Jewish teachings. He established a Jewish school in Addis Abeba and fostered the observance of Torah and commandments in line with the practices of traditional Judaism throughout the world. Following his lead, the Jewish Agency sent emissaries to Ethiopia and established such schools in Asmara, Ambover, Wuzaba and elsewhere.

Much of Faitlovitch's energy was devoted to convincing the Jewish world of the wonder and worthiness of this people, and like Theodor Herzl, he went with hat in hand seeking help everywhere.

His own report to Baron Rothchild and other works contributed to the written record that began to grow rapidly as researchers became aware that much of the fascinating story was yet to be discovered. Major researchers included A.Z. Aescoly published in Jerusalem in 1943, Wolf Leslau, whose prolific works and Amharic dictionaries began appearing in 1945 and still do, and Edward Ullendorff of London University whose works (1955, 1965, 1968) have become standard on the Ethiopians and their language.

In the seventies and eighties the output continued. Max Wurmbrand's article, "The Falashas," in the *Encyclopedia Judaica* is thorough and readily available.

These scholars had recorded and enlarged the contact, but the actual rescue of the Beta Yisrael depended on the attitude and actions of Israel. When Emperor Haile Selassie (who had ruled since 1928) was deposed in 1936 by the Italians, he fled to Jerusalem with his family and staff. In 1941 he marched back victoriously from Sudan. He abstained in the UN Palestine partition vote, but an Israeli Consulate was established in Addis Abeba in 1956, followed by full diplomatic relations by 1961.

The problem was that Israel itself made no significant efforts on behalf of Ethiopian Jewry after achieving statehood in 1948. In the 1960's Professor Norman Bentwich of the Hebrew University tried to get immigration moving, but could not convince the Lion of Judah.

When the Emperor was again deposed in 1974—this time by the revolution —the fate of the remaining Beta Yisrael seemed sealed. The only Jewish organization allowed into Ethiopia was ORT, which ran vocational schools and health services till it was summarily evicted in 1981. This left 19 schools and clinics and synagogues without funds.

Formally, there was equality and the Jews had the "right" even to own land; but the local population would not countenance that, and with the general lack of wherewithal, the Beta Yisrael were reduced to a tenant-farmer status.

A new government policy now seeks to consolidate villages into large units, moving entire populations around to achieve this. This poses a mortal threat to the Beta Yisrael who were able to hold on to their traditions only by remaining separate in small Jewish units.

It was pressure from pro-Falasha organizations in the U.S., Canada, and Britain that moved Israel to sporadic rescue efforts until, by November 1984, over 7,000 Beta Yisrael had reached Israel. Then the incredible Operation Moses (November 24, 1984—January 3, 1985) fueled by famine and death in Ethiopia— added another 7,500 in just a few weeks.

By then, close to 3,000 Ethiopian Jews—mostly children—had perished of hunger, disease, and hardships on the roads and in refugee camps. All 100 members of the U.S. Senate demanded action. On March 3 another airlift took place. Some called it Operation Joshua, others Sheba, but the confusion went beyond that. The people had given up and left the collection points, and only 800 could be flown out.

Since the beginning of 1985, the Beta Yisrael population has remained about evenly divided between Israel and Ethiopia (approximately 16,000 in each). Having sold their oxen, plows and tools in preparation for the journey to the land of promise, those left behind—mostly women, children and the older generation—are vulnerable and impoverished. Those who got out before Operation Moses was tragically disclosed and halted, left with the certainty that the others would follow in a matter of days for a reunion in Jerusalem.

"What did we do?" is their cry in Israel today. "In hindsight, had we known our parents would not get out, would we have gone, even though they urged us on?"

Zivia Lubetkin, forced to flee the burning ghetto of Warsaw in 1943 with a handful of young Jewish fighters, asks the same question even as she moves through the waters of the sewers of Warsaw: "How can we leave them?" And others of the Holocaust asked: "Why did *we* survive?"

The guilt the new Israelis feel is enormous as the separation drags on endlessly. The problems caused by this separation and some of the steps being taken to end it are reflected in the essays at the beginnings of each chapter following and even more dramatically in the photographs themselves—all of which comprise the continuing story.

With the revolutionary regime in power, visiting was made more difficult, until today the villages are entirely closed, even to researchers. Organized tours are sometimes allowed in, but under the watchful eye of government guides who prevent any real contact with the people. Such fleeting and surreptitious touchings as take place are hardly a framework for investigating demographic, cultural and religious changes.

Fortunately, the Beta Yisrael in Israel, still first generation immigrants, provide living testimony that can be measured against the evidence of the early writers. At the same time they are gaining new energy in the climate of freedom and opportunity in Israel—an energy they are using to apply the protest and pressure needed to bring the plight of their sundered families to the attention of the world.

"Must we wait for more famine and deaths before anything is done?" they challenge—an ominous question. The 1984-5 drought, that turned Ethiopia into an immense graveyard where children fell to skin and bones, can return any year and wreak havoc in a land where there is no Joseph to gather and store the grain against the lean years.

Still, the decimated Beta Yisrael have not lost faith and during the famine of 1988 recalled the promise in the prophet's vision of the dry bones:

> *And I will lay sinews upon you, and will bring up flesh*
> *upon you, and cover you with skin, and put breath in you, and*
> *ye shall live... and I will cause you to come up out of your*
> *graves, O My people; and bring you into the land of Israel.*
>
> Ezekiel 37:6,12

The Little Ones

ጨቅላ

cheqla

*When the little ones
    are blessed,
The parents—by that alone—
    are blessed.*
        Book of Splendor, i, 227b

*On the day he first speaks,
    his parents have joy.
When he marries and leaves,
    they cry for that boy!*
        Ethiopian Proverb

The neighboring southern cities of Ashkelon and Gath dating back to Biblical days ("Tell it not in Gath") are home to a large and youthful Ethiopian Jewish community where infants abound. Conditions—the housing, training, work—are a bit trying for the immigrants there, as they are in Beersheba, Netanya, Afula, and Nazareth (travelling south to north), home to the largest concentration of Beta Yisrael in Israel. However, there are many compensations and blessings—the greatest of which are the children themselves. Babies and children up to school age receive the closest attention and love.

Dani, reviver of tales, holds the little ones wrapped in wonder as he tells a long, long fable set in the brush-hills and waters of the lands around Lake Gondar in northwest Ethiopia, where hundreds of Jewish villages have existed for centuries.

23

Unexpectedly, the leopard agrees to let the goat drink from the same river with him—but downstream. At the climax of the tale, the leopard gives up his friendship with the goat for the prospect of making a tasty meal of him. But he is worried and asks the goat casually "Will I be punished if I...if I...uh...do something wrong?" "I don't think so," answers the goat, "but I have heard that your children will probably be punished for your sins." That seems fair to the leopard, and he leaps at the goat to devour him, deciding his children could fend for themselves. He was hungry now.

Alas, he leaps too high and is impaled on the pointed branch of a tree. "I thought you said my children would be punished for their father's sins, not I," wails the leopard. "Even so," the bearded goat nods wisely, "but apparently your father has sinned as well."

The dreams of the Ethiopian *cheqlas* (infants through toddlers) pictured in the following pages may still be filled with leopards and goats and regretfully, the nasty hyena as well, when mother or grandmother remember the old stories; but the real world that passes them by beyond the crib or carriage moves today at the pace of bikes and cars and the rhythms of Israel's TV version of Sesame Street.

"The sins of the fathers are visited upon their children" is countered in Jewish teaching by the concept of "the Merit of the Fathers," through which the good deeds of Abraham and Sarah and all parents enure to the benefit of their children. (It is the good that lives on in the Jewish view and is not "interred with their bones" as the Bard of Avon would have it.)

The good deeds of the parents of these Beta Yisrael children were heroic in epic proportions. Their parents brought these children to Israel literally on their backs, by walking for months over hills and rocks, through heat and scrub and keeping them alive in sprawling refugee camps in the Sudan where death for many of the young and old came easier than life. Some parents, too weak for the ordeal, made an even greater sacrifice and stayed behind letting others carry their precious ones away from them. As many as 1500 youngsters in Israel thus are still orphaned by separation. Some of these parents had no choice... and perished on the way.

The Exodus of over seven thousand Jews out of Ethiopia at the end of 1984 and into 1985 was aptly named Operation Moses. But the waters did not part miraculously for these parents and children, and the sands of the Sudanese desert proved a more implacable foe than the waters of the Red Sea.

A deeper question then. How did the frail, half-starved mothers make it with their little ones on their backs—while some women and men with no one to carry fell and arose no more.

The Jews, experts in Holocaust, have supplied an answer to this question long ago. Martyrdom was another bond between the Ethiopian Jews and their fellow Jews whom they knew not. How did the Jews survive the centuries? One of the most frequent answers is—The Torah sustained them. "The Ark carried its bearers" is the way the rabbis put it.

Here, too, it was the little ones who bore their parents. For their sake they just had to remain upright and walking, climbing over the rocks and down to the fearsome sands and surviving through the hell of "the Mother of Death," as the largest and worst of the Sudanese camps was called. They had to, for if they faltered, the little ones would perish.

24

These then are not just ordinary infants that you will meet on the following pages. These little ones came to Israel by a special grace—even those who were born here—through the Merit of their Mothers who strove mightily to reach a new land.

Every land is new for the newborn, as it is for the children whose parents leave the homeland. How will the newly arrived and the newly born ever know that they are different from all other Jewish Ethiopian babies born before them? How much will they ever know of the "old country"?

They will never really known a *tukul*—the wattled grass homes in which their brothers and sisters were raised. They will never know the crowds and the fun of market day in Tedda or Ambover, or the pain or rejection when the man won't buy your little "genuine" Solomon and Sheba ceramic statues. They will never be *cheqlas*—unpampered little ones, carefully instructed in their duties and ancient ways and traditions as soon as they are old enough to learn.

Baby is nursed for about two years and acquires strong feelings of security, special feelings, awarded only those carried about in an *ankelba* on mother's back. Later, the child learns to bow and kiss the knees of elders to show respect. Vestiges of the gesture remain throughout life, even in Israel today. It may be that the evident quality of restraint in emotions and deeds came from living in a hostile environment where affability and agreeability were protective necessities. Whatever the cause, the gentle characteristics remain and are readily observed and appreciated.

Isn't it a wonder that our babies who are diapered and powdered and watched over incessantly often grow up brash and demanding... while the *cheqla*—fed, bathed, back-packed, yet often left to fend for itself—turned into a paragon of politeness, cooperation and diffidence. Well, that's freedom. That's what they came to a "modern country" for, to grow into saucy little *sabras*. Maybe a bit of both worlds will stick to them and they will grow up to be special people—just as they were when they were born.

Did I not give thee hands to touch with...

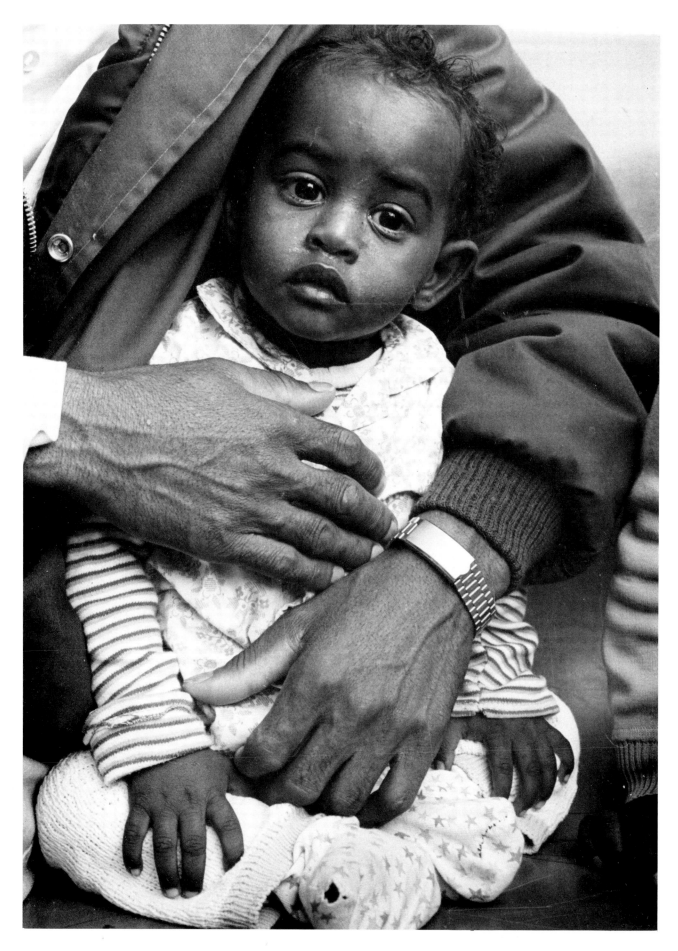

...and a heart with which to think!

The Book of Angels

And the Lord will recover the remnant of His people… and from Cush (Ethiopia)… and will assemble the dispersed of Israel… from the four corners of the earth.

Isaiah 11:11-12

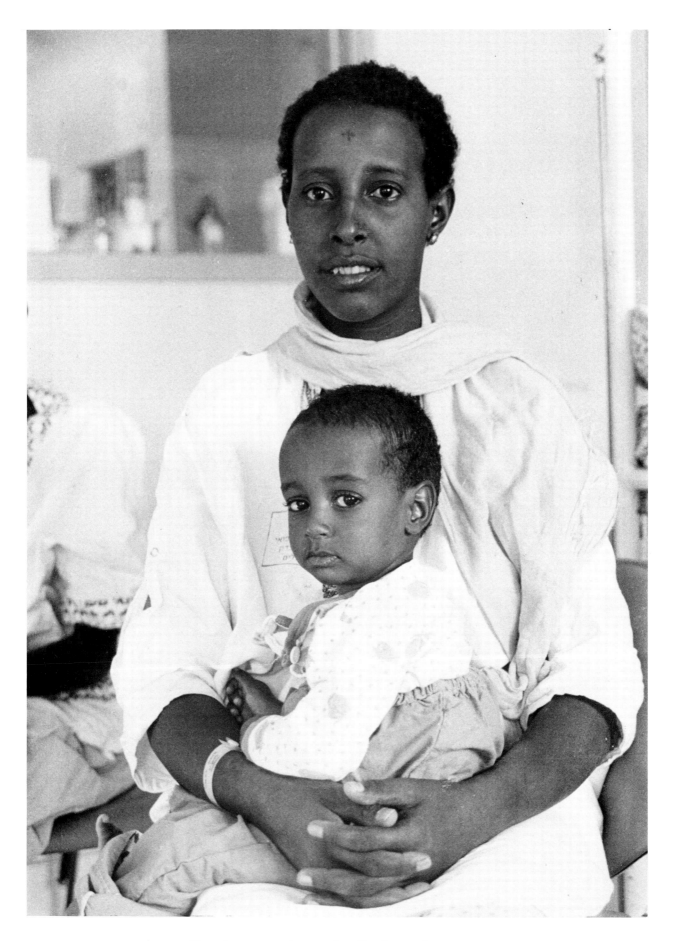

Her demeanor bespeaks dignity and grace —
Her heart speaks love —

New arrival… *in* Israel

New arrival... *to* Israel—January 4, 1985
Towelled...
Turbanned...
and Tagged...

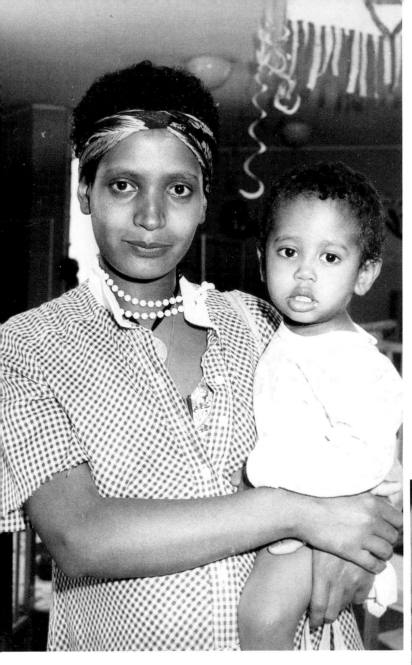

Israeli Style

Both women are raising a family and are enrolled in programs to acquire a productive skill.

"Oh yes, we do look different here... and we feel different too."

"With our children prattling in Hebrew, we have to. In one way, our little ones have a head start over the other *sabras*, they're bilingual."

"A place we can leave the little ones so we can work, study, and become mothers in a modern world."

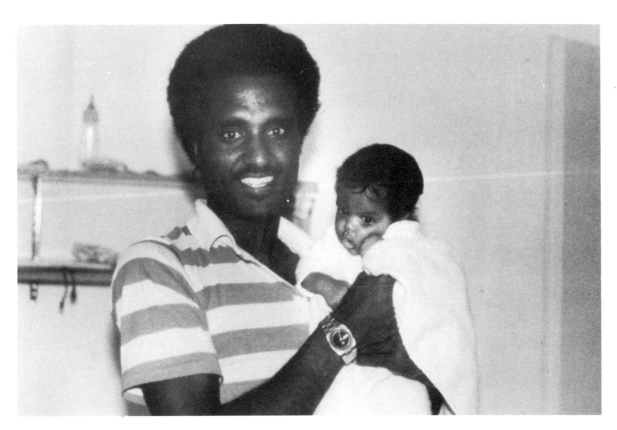

A few days after the family arrived in Israel, mother gave birth to this little girl. So delighted and grateful were they that they named her *Yisrael* (Israel). Several weeks later, in their Hebrew language class, they discovered that Yisrael is a masculine name and is never given to a girl!

"Were we still in Ethiopia at the mountain brook near our village, mother would be bathing, and washing the clothes of my eight brothers and sisters, and my clothes and me. There the water would be bubbly with spray. So lovely.

Oh well. You can have a fun splash in this thing, too."

The water supply in "this thing" is a bit more reliable. During 1984—and other years of periodic drought—even the mountain brooks ran dry, and baby could well have been amongst the thousands who perished from disease, hunger and thirst.

So frequently were Beta Yisrael at the stream washing and purifying themselves, that they were known as "Those Who Smell of Water." At the approach of Sabbaths and Festivals, after menstruation and childbirth, after touching a stranger or the food of an outsider and the long list of *tooma*, the defilements in the Five Books of Moses, the people would cleanse themselves at the water, often for days.

"Some of our parents are here —
Some didn't make it.

That's all right,
don't worry
about us—
unless you
want to."

Mother, aged twenty one, with her sons at an immigrant absorption center in southern Israel.

David, aged two, was born in the Sudan, in a sprawling refugee camp. He has already flown in several jets... and had to do some walking too. Does his mien reflect the burdens of his trials?

Yitzchak, shown at six months, was born in Israel, in a modern hospital in Ashkelon. A *sabra* and already laughing at us.

"Lucky for me, mother brought the *ankelba* in which to carry me around. The old ways come in handy in Israel, too."

There is a time to be born...
And a time to laugh...
A time to embrace...
A time to love...

He hath made everything beautiful
In its time.

Ecclesiastes 3:2-11

PRESSBURGER
1987

Childhood

ልጅነት

lijinnet

Train a child in the way he should take, and when he is old, he will not depart from it.

Book of Proverbs 22:6

Learn,
and you will be honored.

Ethiopian Proverb

The pretty, smiling, well-dressed children you meet here are a dream come true. This is exactly how mother would have dressed her little girls in Gondar had a bag of gold coins dropped from heaven (as it does sometimes in the stories back there.) Here in Israel, she can dress the children up without miracles—and almost without money ... with an assist from government agencies and caring people.

While the attempt is to have the kids look as much as possible like their Israeli peers, there is a reluctance to give up former images and identities entirely. The giveaway is the length of the girls' dresses, very much in for those who could afford it in Ethiopia, but a bit out of place in jean and jumper oriented Israel.

What a difference from the hole-pocked rags that seemed mandatory weekday wear for the small fry in Tedda, Aba Entonis or any of the some 500 villages in which distinguishable Jewish communities resided in the Gondar and Tigre provinces. The ragamuffin appearance was tailored to the tasks at hand. The little girl may begin with the sheep, but she soon is guided to home and fireplace to learn pottery work and basketry. Her brother's chores are out in the field where he begins chasing the birds away from the seed. He then is taught the skills of plowing and planting, till he has turned into a farmer like his father or an ironsmith or weaver, special skills of the Jews.

The impoverished appearance of little Anatmar or Yeshiwork arouses pity and helps her sell mother's basketware or ceramic figures (turned out for a time at the Wolleka Pottery Factory). Tesfai, Issaius and Baruch are playing stick and stone games, running, and soon begin practicing on the *dulla* stick, which will someday give attackers pause or help drive off the professional robbers, called *shiftas*. The boys also throw stones for fun or defense, developing throwing arms that later amazed the promoters of Little League Baseball in Israel!

These skills taught character, discipline, and respect for father and mother as teachers and models. Their effects are still visible on many of the children who are growing up as at least hyphenated Israelis. There are deeper marks on the children that you may discern in a pained face or a distrustful glance. Most of these the children are unaware of, but they are there, grooved into the memory of parents and finding echoes in little Ethiopian children, somewhat in the manner of the scars we find on children of Holocaust survivors.

Rachel is one of the most fetching of the little girls on the following pages. Her father says he will tell her his story when she is older. Meanwhile, you see her smiling and bright-eyed, growing ever more secure as school and home routines of the new life in Israel prove recurring and dependable. By the time he tells it, she may be able to handle her father's tale quite well.

In 1955, her father leaves Ethiopia with the approval of Emperor Haile Selassie for schooling in Israel as one of 12 students, aged 11 to 17. In all, 37 boys and girls are sent. They study at the Kfar Batya religious youth village and in due course return to teach the children of Beta Yisrael.

Father is sent to a school in Ambover where he teaches Hebrew and the culture of the Jews of rest of the world. Unofficially, but actually, he is preparing his students for *aliya* a "going up"—as tradition views immigration to Israel.

When he first arrived in his village, he was greeted in joy and exultation. He, one of them, had been to Jerusalem and returned bringing the Torah "out of Zion." The joy was short-lived, as promised help and guidance from Israel was forgotten. Still, father continued to teach and to send letters to Jews in other countries describing pressures from church and government and persecutions that could obliterate the remaining Beta Yisrael community.

In 1974 the Emperor was deposed by a military junta. The horrors of street battles in Addis Abeba spilled over to the villages as terrible excesses. The controlling Committee, the Dergue, took total power as a Marxist regime actively supported by the Soviets and Cuba. How a tribal country, largely monophysite Christian, with heavy Moslem populations in the south, could be converted to Marxism overnight is something the regime is still trying to explain.

In the villages, the Jews felt their status as Falasha—stranger, unwanted element—more keenly than ever. In the midst of the turmoil and oppression, the school teachers were arrested. "They remembered we had studied in Israel. We must be spies," father narrates.

"I cannot describe in words the torture all of us endured there in the prison. I'll try to tell just one example, when they tied me up, my hands behind my back and then pushed my head into a barrel of dirty (sometimes hot) water. Just before I drowned, they would let me out and question me and torture me in in other ways."

"I prayed they would let me drown," said father. "Whether you believe in the Lord of Israel or that there is a guiding purpose to the history of the Jewish people, you have to believe in some power that makes me stand today in freedom in the Land of Israel and in the very same place, Kfar Batya, where I had studied as a boy to tell you all this. Of course, I am deeply grateful to the American Jews who rescued me and brought my family to a second chance in Israel; but they couldn't have done it alone. There is a higher purpose to all this."

The reunion of 8 of the teacher prisoners at the place where it all began made believers of all who beheld it. Standing under a flowering oleander, father looked around the green landscape and saw his nephew, one of a large group of 12 to 13 year olds who were just beginning in the same school where he had studied long ago.

What does it mean to these boys transplanted from Ethiopia that they are studying in an Israeli school?

Back there, most of them would not have gone to school at all. Schools were so far away, and it took the hardiest to manage the long walk. But the hardiest were the ones father needed for the farm... and if you were a girl, what did you need school for?

Back there, if you did get to school, you faced deep prejudice and fear of the Falasha. You were *buda*, a bad omen, an evil eye. You were kin to the ironworkers who made evil sparks of hell fly that could bring destruction. At night, you could change yourself into a body-eating hyena.

The dangers were real—from robbers to rapists to those who would spirit you away to the army when you grew up a bit. From the army you rarely returned.

Life has its cares in Israel too. There really isn't quite enough of anything in these early years when parents are trying to find their way as new immigrants and their place in a demanding society.

Rachel, though, really doesn't worry about things like that. Life is just beautiful in Israel and school is a marvelous place. If you just try a little, teacher is so pleased. Actually, greatly pleased, as the children have turned out to be bright and quick, eager to learn and well-behaved.

They have songs in school, picture drawing and games and outings, too, if *ennat* (mother) can find the fee. We can have ice cream and play marbles if the boys let us... and some of our own games, if we remember them. Sometimes it seems we can remember, and sometimes it seems as if there were good moments there too.

"As for the things that happened to my father, I can't worry about them, because... he hasn't told me yet."

Exiled to Babylonia with the destruction of the Second Temple in 586 BCE, the Jewish community flourished there for over 1,000 years. Like the Beta Yisrael, they too were scattered in Jewish settlements over a well-defined area. Among the many differences was the fact that the Babylonians maintained contact with Palestine and all of the Jewish world, while in Abyssinia, the Beta Yisrael thought themselves to be the only Jews left in the world.

The Babylonian Talmud tells us (*Hullin, 24*) that the great sage, Rabbah, often bought imperfect earthenware for his little ones to break if they wished, "for their development," he said. Surely Beta Yisrael mothers who sustain their children by making and selling ceramics have plenty of chipped pottery dolls around and undoubtedly follow the Rabbi's advice without ever having heard it. Other Talmudic wisdoms would also come naturally to Beta Yisrael fathers such as,

Do not threaten a child. Punish him or forgive him.

Smahot 2,6

If you must strike a child, use a shoestring.

Baba Batra, 21

45

In a Hassidic tale, "Susia is Hungry," a coincidence makes it appear as if the Almighty Himself provides Susia's breakfast, just as the Rebbe expected. In a Beta Yisrael tale, the husband insists that "G-d will provide for our children," and refuses to help his wife carry home a huge jug full of silver coins she found in the forest. "G-d will bring it to us," he insists.

She gets a stranger to help. Cunningly, he tells her to wait till morning. At midnight he drags the jug to his own home, opens it and finds a huge snake within.

Furious, he lugs it up onto the lady's roof and hurls the jug and snake down into her house. Whereupon a shower of silver coins fills her home.

"See?" crows her husband. "I told you that G-d would deliver it!"

In the hills, near Jerusalem

The bus is going somewhere

Operation Moses

November 1984—January 1985

In the beginning it wasn't easy

It was all slightly bewildering at first... but when the Festival of Lights brought songs and goodies and gifts for everyone, it turned out to be a good time to arrive in Israel after all.

Hanukkah—a "new" holiday for Beta Yisrael (as it is not in the Bible) with an old blessing that seemed just right for them as well:
"We thank Thee for the miraculous and mighty deeds of liberation wrought by Thee, and for Thy victories in the battles our forefathers fought in days of old, at this season of the year."
...The Prayerbook

He: Back home umbrellas were for the men.
She: This is a parasol... and this is Israel!

*The world itself rests
upon the breath of the children
in the schoolhouse of their teachers...*
Talmud, Shabbat 119b

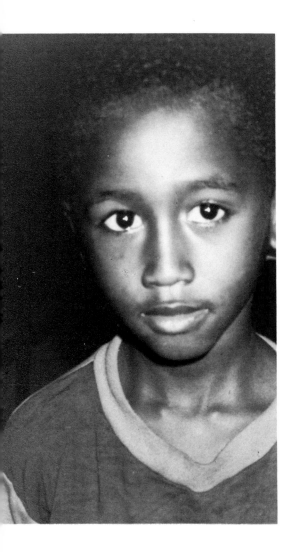

Bright eyes, set in bright faces of the Children of Israel in many places throughout the Land of Israel...

A most literal realization of the Prophecy of Jeremiah (24:6)

I will set mine eyes upon them for good,
And I will bring them back to this land...

ዓይኑን፡አፍጥጦ

aynun aft'it'o
"wide eyes"

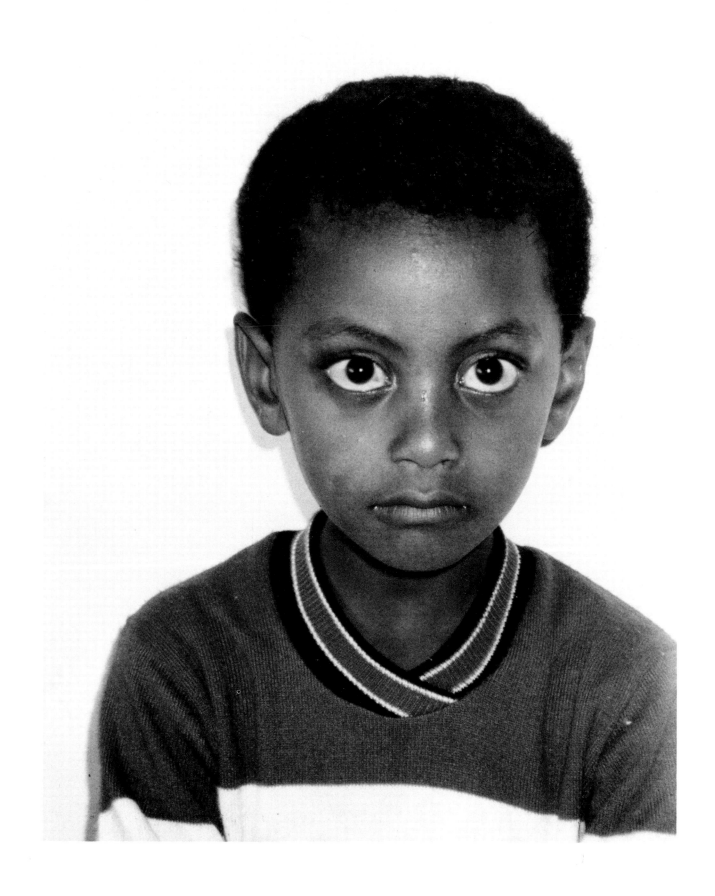

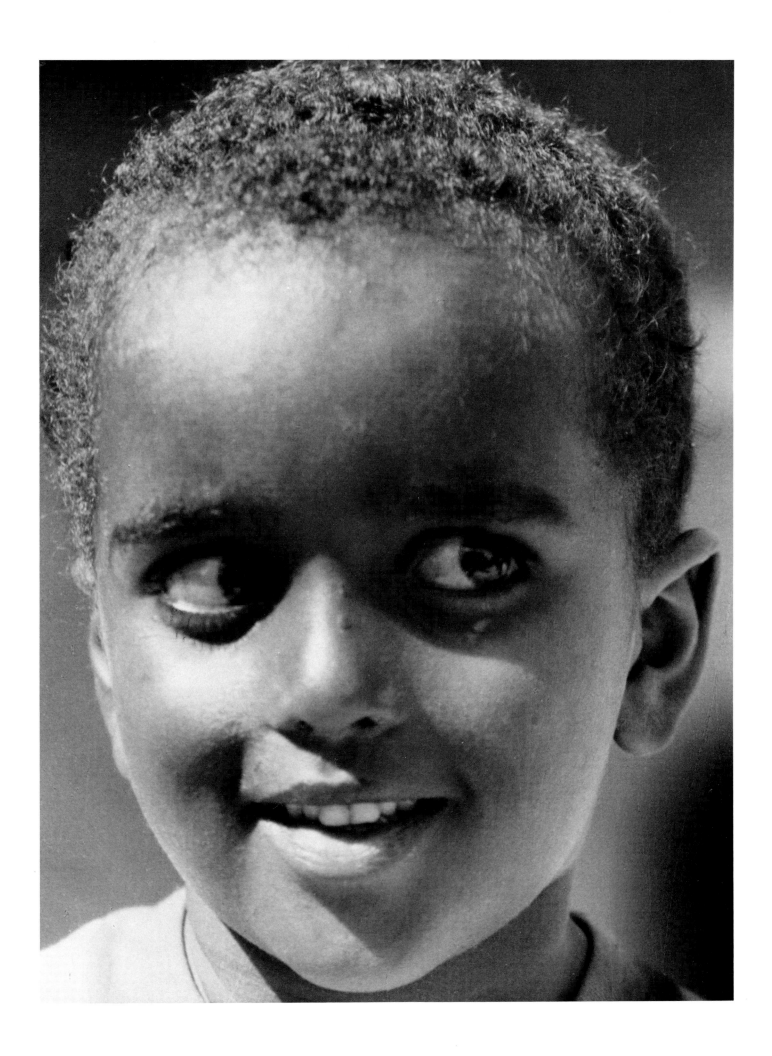

In Afula

In Safed

In Jerusalem

In Netanya

57

Things swing up and
things swing down...
but at this age
there's plenty of fun in Israel.

Four children, two boys and two girls, with mother and father complete a happy family of six.

Now, mother's sister and son have arrived and there are eight in the small apartment.

"Less room, but more joy!" mother says.

Adult worries do not seep down to the children who are shown happy in the center and carefree in the corners.

Looking down
from the top of the world

Climbing in Liberty Bell Park

And just rolling along in Or Akiva

61

He who learns, teaches
Ethiopian Proverb

A Heavy Responsibility

Talk of primitivism of the immigrants from a backward country is still heard occasionally—but not from anyone who has had significant contact with them, and certainly not from any of their teachers.

Some 1500 youngsters came without family. The man in charge of the villages and schools that house them knows them best and speaks with authority... and love:

"...I was besieged by the 'experts' who insisted that the Ethiopians are so backward that there was no point in making them literate. Teaching them 1,000 words of spoken Hebrew should be enough... They should be sent out on the job market as soon as could be to make them less of a burden on the taxpayer.

Another 'expert' suggestion was to lower the standard of schooling for the Ethiopian youth.

This too was categorically ruled out. We have enormously motivated kids here. Unlike some of our *sabras* who pray their teacher will be sick and miss a day of school, the Ethiopian youngsters get to class early in the hope that the lesson will start before the bell. They also study far into the night, after dormitory lights are supposed to be out.

Regard these *olim* (immigrants) with a little less arrogance. We seem to forget the difference between technological advancement and cultural values. The Ethiopians may be ignorant about satellite communications, but they could teach us a thing or two about family love."

At a Hanukkah celebration

Young Ladies

At home in Netanya

The trophy is almost as tall as Tuvia, but he is a big man at second base. He handles the ball well, hits 300 and is a relief pitcher.

He's a surprise player to everyone but his mother.

"If only his father could join us here," she says. "He's still in the village. He had to let us go first... and then they closed everything tight."

Watch out for Gideon! He smiles a lot, but swings a mean bat. He's a deaf mute and has the advantage of not hearing the coach's shouting to let the bad pitches go by. He swings at everything and usually connects with solid doubles.

The star of the team is Zvi, a stone thrower back in the village. He hurled a no-hitter and a one-hitter in the 1987 season.

Even as he zips in fast-ball strikes, moroseness seems permanently etched into his expression. Zvi is featured in a video documentary, and his suffering look is fully explained as he talks about his mother and his seven brothers and sisters.

"And where is your father?"

"He died... back there."

The winning Netanya team has five Beta Yisrael players in the starting line-up, plus a boy from Russia and three Israel born youngsters.

In 1987, ten teams from around the country vied for the first Israel-America Little League Pennant. The first ball was thrown out in the opener by Mayor Teddy Kollek in Jerusalem, and the first trophy was presented at season's end to the team in Netanya. Not one of the players had ever seen a baseball bat seven months earlier. The Ethiopians had never been on a sports team of any kind before in their lives.

ז"ל

In Loving Memory

December 1986
Four year old Rachel lights her last Hanukkah candle.

The following June her brief life was suddenly snuffed out in a bizarre accident in an elevator.

She was a child of great beauty and promise and the entire Beta Yisrael community in Israel was in shock and mourning.

In a moving tribute to her memory, two thousand Jews of the Ethiopian community gathered in love, mourning and determination to bring life to all of this ancient Community in the Land where Abraham and Sarah worshipped "The Lord of all the families of Israel." (Jeremiah . 31.1)

What lies ahead?

When these girls were born, the happy family called out in joy the traditional nine times. For the boys it was twelve.

The female child, *set lij* in Amharic, is soon concerned with school, teachers, friends, games... and dresses and parties, as is the beauty on the next page. There is normalcy. There is childhood. There is reason for joy in Israel.

It is hard to believe... but it is a fact of their lives that Beta Yisrael will not soon forget (and will pass on to their children when they are older) that in the year 1984 (yes, *"1984,"* curiously also the year *tashmad* on the Hebrew calendar indicating destruction), little girls the age of those pictured here were part of the mass escape from Ethiopia.

They were good walkers, and since they had been raised to respect and trust their elders uncomplainingly, they wimpered or cried in silence as they walked for day after day after day with little food and less water... and though many perished, even more survived both the journey and the horrendous conditions in the teeming refugee camps.

For those who made it to the day (it was night actually) when they boarded a plane that eventually reached Israel, then were cured of a host of diseases in an Israeli hospital—for these plucky survivors, it is permissible for you to add three more cheers of joy.

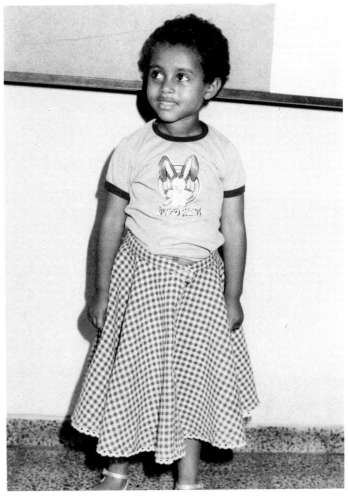

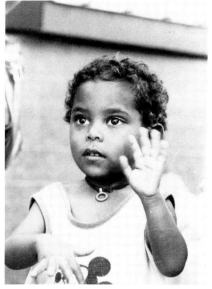

"Teacher says
I learn so quickly
I could be a professor."

"Mother says
I can be anything I want to
in Israel."

"I don't know.
Grandmother keeps saying
You are beautiful, beautiful!"

"Do you think I could be on television?"

Welcoming New York Mayor Ed Koch at an absorption center.
A few months later, Vice President Bush came.
"If important people come to see us—we must be important."

Love

The Time of Fire

እሳት

ye-isat gize

Behold thou art fair, my love.
Song of Songs 1:15

Love to the grave.
Ethiopian Saying

Up the hills and down the vales, amidst the trees in the soft rolling slopes in and about the Jewish villages surrounding Lake Tana, a young man might be reprimanded for sexual indiscretions and certainly for fathering a child out of wedlock, but he, and also his father, could make amends.

Anyway, he had no test to pass. He was the same now as before. There was no prohibition in the *Orit* (the Torah in an ancient translation), as long as the girl was unattached.

Anyway, he was in the "Time of Fire," uncontrolled, passionate. Everybody knew that. So he was understood, and there wasn't all that much trouble for him.

Anyway, she wouldn't tell. If she did, she condemned herself. For the young woman, not "telling" could protect her only until she was to marry. Of course, the wise old women had already examined her before the wedding. They could swear

to the priest that she was a virgin. But if they wouldn't, the groom would tear off the *keshera*, the white and red headband that the *qes* had tied on him, and her shame and inquisition would begin. She would have to tell who did it... and then...

73

It wasn't like that anymore in Israel.

He had so many involvements, responsibilities, studies, jobs, that the "Time of Fire" was no longer all-consuming. Just keeping up with school, making ends meet and keeping his bank account straight was fire enough.

She, on the other hand, was actually more exposed in the new society than she had been in the old. There the strongest taboos helped her out, and with early marriage it wasn't all that hard to make it intact to the wedding bed.

Everything seems more difficult in Israel. Far from the old rural setting, getting married is suddenly an ordeal, surrounded with red tape, witnesses to prove your eligibility, struggles for a proper apartment of your own, and the all-important job for her betrothed.

Here, equalities and freedoms were thrust upon her that she had not known. She could move anywhere on her own, well outside the protecting family circle. After high school, she was largely separated from her cousins and closest friends. In a training course or at work, strangers surrounded her. Whether they projected a desire to help or just curiosity, they made her feel so uncomfortable. The self-assured young men looked at her as if she were the Queen of Sheba.

The transition had been too sudden. How had it all begun? How had she come to be here, a showpiece in this strange land that bore the name of her people and was its ancestral homeland?

I am black,
and beautiful.
We are daughters of Jerusalem.

Song of Songs 1:5

Solomon, King of Israel, parades the beauty of young women and young men as the centerpiece of his dramatic poem, *The Song of Songs* (1:15,16)...

> He: *Behold, thou art fair my love, behold thou art fair.*
> *Thine eyes are as doves.*
> She: *Behold, thou art fair my beloved and pleasant,*
> *and our couch is leafy.*

In the book of First Kings (Chapter 10) that recounts the history of Solomon, the Bible tells us:

> *...And when the Queen of Sheba* (Ethiopia) *heard the fame of*
> *Solomon... she came to Jerusalem.*
> *...And King Solomon gave to the Queen of Sheba all her desire,*
> *whatever she asked, besides which Solomon gave her of his royal bounty.*

His "royal bounty" included gifts of great munificence, and "all her desire" was more than enough basis for the firmly held belief since time immemorial in Ethiopia that Solomon put her in way of child.

The child is a son, Menelik, founder of the royal dynasty, who thus ties the Emperors of Ethiopia to Solomon, to the Bible of the Hebrews and to the Land of the Jews. This legend is fixed in popular belief and moves the Star of David as a symbol through the centuries till it comes to crown the last of the line, the Negus (Emperor) Haile Selassie, the "Lion of Judah."

The legend then expands itself to explain (if legends can explain) the presence of black Jews in Abyssinia who cling to the teachings of the Torah of Moses. Menelik grows up and naturally seeks his origins. Would he not want to go to Jerusalem to his father, to pay homage and to receive blessing and recognition?

He would, had he been taught the words his mother spoke to Solomon as recorded in the Book of Kings: *"Blessed be the Lord thy G-d, who delighted in thee, to set thee on the throne of Israel; because the Lord loved Israel forever, therefore made He thee king, to do justice and righteousness."* (I Kings 10:9)

So deep was the love of his mother for this religion of righteousness that she at once presents Solomon with *"120 talents of gold... a great store of spices... and precious stones."* (ibid 10:10)

So Menelik visits his father, then returns to Ethiopia, but not empty handed. He brings with him many Israelites, some Kohanim and Levites. A bit ungratefully, however, the legend has him smuggle the Ark of the Covenant and the Tablets bearing the Law and transfers them from Jerusalem to Aksum, which is his capital in ancient Abyssinia.

Being oldest, this legend has no external corroboration yet fits the subsequent development of Beta Yisrael in Ethiopia quite as well as later theories adduced to explain their presence there through documented paths and moves of the games anthropologists play.

Though the Beta Yisrael didn't know about the rest of the Jewish world, the Jews, and especially biblical exegetes, knew of them. Jewish folklore contains a fantastic story that Moses fled to the land of Cush, as Ethiopia is called in the Bible, after killing the Egyptian taskmaster to become a distinguished soldier in the army of King Kikonos. So brave and beautiful was he, that the people wanted to crown him king on the death of Kikonos.

Israelis are shocked to see quiet and shy Beta Yisrael girls do what looks like the bump and grind, and shaking in a most provocative way, while young men do violent, though controlled, shoulder dances. Both dance and music, the beat of the drum and the sounds of the one-stringed lute and the lyre, seem harsh and discordant to the western ear. Yet these have proven themselves potentials of contact and a bridge to understanding. So strong and solid was the drum beat, so stark and vivid the story of the leopard and the hunter being danced with vigor on an Israeli stage recently, that some 500 Israeli youth were completely caught up in the dangers of the hunt and quickly joined the dancers in the ever-more-frenzied cry of the warning refrain.

The tape recorder is one of the first acquisitions of the youths who reach Israel. Tapes are transmitted through France and Italy and lyrics and music have an Addis Abeba, big city sound. They obviously generate nostalgia, comfort, and thoughts of "home" amongst youth, though most of them were country kids back there.

Historically, the Jews of Ethiopia have been socially quite isolated from their neighbors. Religious practices, including a strong belief that contact brings defilement, physical separation of the village or a quarter within it and the concomitant hostility toward them by the dominant group, all tended to emphasize and preserve cultural differences.

It was somewhat in the way Jews of the Polish *shtetel* kept aloof from the gentile and thanked G-d for the walls of the ghetto as much as they cursed them.

Those walls finally cracked through varies stages of emancipation in Western, then Eastern Europe. A common language and environment and the communication gadgets of modern times have broken barriers in some areas in Ethiopia as well. Music is an obvious one and dance which is its handmaid.

This "Wedding Song," far from the spirit of the *Song of Songs*, describes an Ethiopian, but non-Jewish courtship. With the Beta Yisrael all arrangements were conducted by father, and *he* would be demanding the fine toga for his daughter. As for her kicking the shins... *"Abbet, abbet!"* (Heaven forbid!)

WEDDING SONG

O *bridegroom*, rejoice!
Your bride is charming!
Your bride is a carafe,
Take care not to break her.
  Lala shebo,
  Lala shebo!

If they ask what you drink
Tell them fresh milk and honey.
If they ask what you eat,
Tell them hump of the bull.
  Lala shebo,
  Lala shebo!

O listen, *bride*, listen:
If they ask you, you say
That you are of a good clan,
Both father and mother.
  Lala shebo,
  Lala shebo!

A fast mule to ride,
A fine toga to wear.
If they can't afford these,
Kick their shins and come home!
  Lala shebo,
  Lala shebo!

Shinega's Village by Sahle Sellassie

Slowly, the young Beta Israel realize that what they achieve will determine the quality of their life and the future of their entire community in Israel. Slowly they begin finding their place and moving up. They are the first to master Hebrew. Many of them are taking courses, some of which are quite technical and difficult, to be able to support themselves and integrate into this society. Many are in different kinds of schools as well as universities. Many are in the Army—a good transitional experience. Many are already working. All are trying.

They have been tested, analyzed, watched, judged, and headlined. They have borne it all with characteristic patience and slowly and determinedly kept moving ahead. They have often been aided and encouraged by veteran Israelis and many have been "adopted" by families who thought they would be largely giving, but were often surprised to see how much they received from these alert and motivated young people.

> *Behold, I have refined thee but not in* (a crucible for) *silver,*
> *I have tested thee in the furnace of affliction.*

Isaiah's words (48:10) often have special meaning for the Beta Yisrael. All in all, even as they are being tried in the crucible, it is evident that they are coming through, strengthened and enriched from this, their Time of Fire.

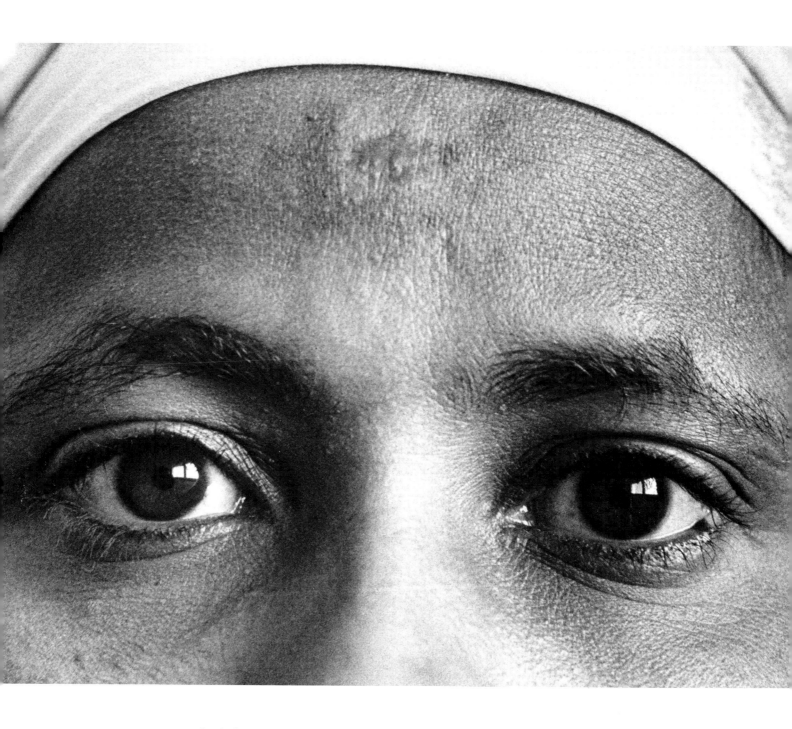

And the eyes of them that see shall not be dim.

Isaiah 32:3

From Ethiopia to Israel
    ...a plane or two...
    ...a day or two...
      It's not far...
      But the psychological, social, and cultural journey is huge.

          From the Bible

To the 20th Century.

Her ways are ways
of pleasantness…
Proverbs 3:17

Studying   Hadayot Youth Village in Galilee, 1987

and Relaxing   Hebrew Ulpan in Ashkelon Absorption Center, 1985

Getting Into It

The time and the place demand a great change for the Beta Yisrael women.

Some are already professionals—

Some are students in university and teachers' colleges—

Many are in special and practical courses, amongst the most popular being nursing, dental assistant, computers, bookkeeping, childcare, hotel work, and dressmaking.

It's quite distinctive and surprisingly in fashion, to wear your Beta Yisrael best to a friend's wedding... or anywhere.

In many ways the Beta Yisrael seem to be biblical people, transported to our day. Thus the prophet's description seems quite apt here:

And she was a woman of good understanding and of a beautiful countenance...

First Samuel: 25:3

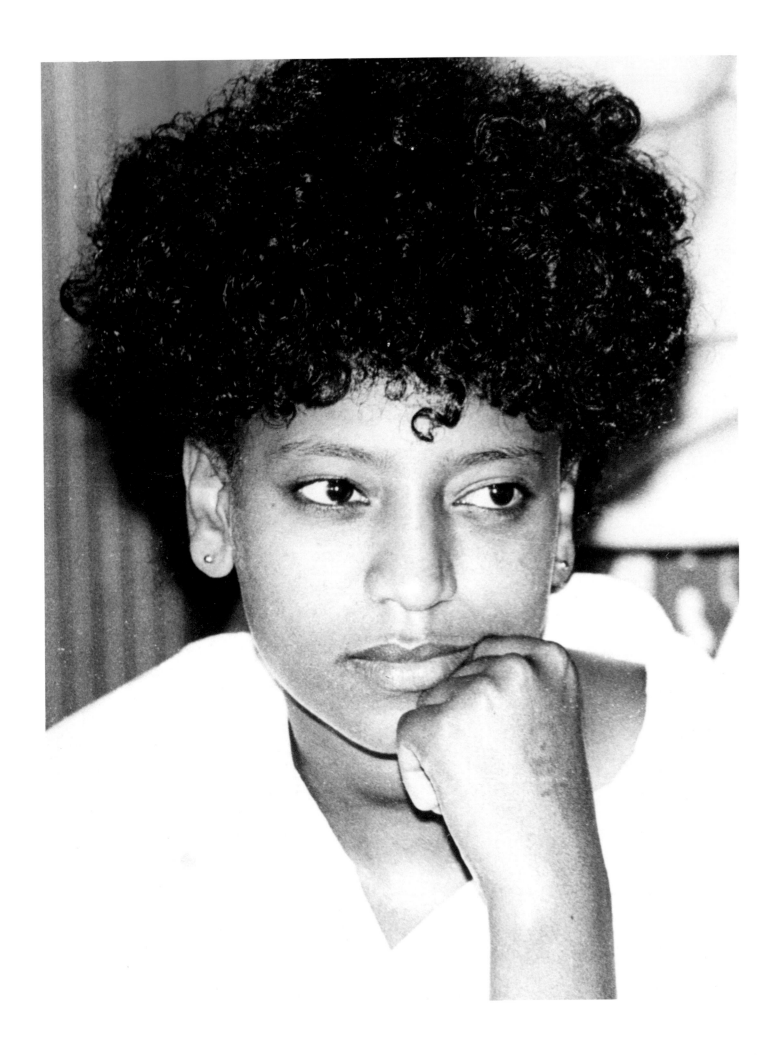

Popular Assembly for the Reunification of Ethiopian Jewish Families

*The Assembly will be held at the Binyanei Hauma, Jerusalem,
Monday, July 27, 1987, I Av 5747, 6:00 P.M.*

Chairman:
In the Presence of:

Knesset Speaker Shlomo Hillel
Prime Minister Yitzhak Shamir
Absorption Minister Yaakov Tsur
Knesset Members
Representatives of
    Divided Ethiopian Families
Keynote Speech — Natan Sharansky
Prof. Erwin Cotler

Musical Program:

Dance Troupe of the Association
of Ethiopian Immigrants
Corrine Alal
Habrera Hativit
Arieh Alias
Danny Shoshan and Kimal
Rivka Zohar   and others...

Master of Ceremonies:

Avraham Burg
Orly Yaniv

Director and Producer:

Yossi Alfi and Orit Zarmi

Public Invited!!

23, Hillel St., Jerusalem. Tel. (02)248722

Joint Rescue Committee
For Ethiopian Jews

Representatives of
Divided Families

Association of Ethiopian
Immigrants in Israel

While the elders are highly respected and honored, the leadership of the Beta Yisrael is in the hands of young people, like those shown in the following pages.

Only they have mastered the Hebrew tongue of the Prophets and only they have the stamina and determination to carry on the struggle to unite their sundered families... to work or study all day, then to meet and plan all night.

The Call Goes Out

...Letters to the Government and leaders of Israel—

...Letters to ambassadors, U.N. officials, even Presidents of foreign lands—

...and always, always to mother or father and loved ones who are keeping the Vigil under most trying circumstances back in Ethiopia.

The *Menorah*, the seven-branched candelabrum, is a symbol of Jewish unity and ingathering of the exiles. Across the plaza from the Knesset, Israel's parliament, it was the site of a 40-day Vigil in the summer of 1987, aimed at pressing for the release of the remaining 16,000 Jews left behind in Ethiopia.

Under the slogan of Family Reunification, the appeal went out to such nations of the world as might be willing to exert pressures on the Ethiopian Government to allow families split in half to unite again in Israel as a simple humanitarian act.

87

FACES
AT THE
VIGIL

Summer 1987

Every spare moment
spent at
the Vigil advocating
Family Reunification.

The People Gather

How long? cries Moses to the despot in the biblical drama. (Exodus 10:13)

"How long" echo the Beta Yisrael on July 27, 1987, at a rally in Jerusalem where thousands of Israelis from all over the country filled the capitol's huge Convention Center.

They heard the Prime Minister and involved officials promise to work for redemption for their families by completing the Exodus.

The very next verses in Exodus (14,15,16) can be read as a powerful warning to Ethiopia: *"If thou refuse to let my people go, behold tomorrow I will bring locusts into thy border. And they shall cover the face of the earth, and they shall eat... everything that groweth for you out of the field, as neither thy father nor thy fathers' fathers have seen... unto this day."*

About 3250 years later, during the 40-day Vigil, the BBC Africa service reported the heaviest mass of swarms of locusts in Ethiopia in modern times waiting for such a confluence of wind and natural phenomena as is usually thought to be the providence of the Almighty Himself.

Inside the National Convention Center, Jerusalem

Next Year In Jerusalem

"Ad Matai?" the tag reads—"How Long?"

Meanwhile—Life Goes On…

Rabbi Yosef Hadane, the only Ethiopian who has completed a full course of classical Jewish studies and has been ordained in Israel as a fully recognized Rabbi. In this he does not follow in the footsteps of his highly respected father, a *qes* who serves Beta Yisrael here in the ways and traditions of Jewish life as it was in Ethiopia.

Hadane means the Danite, attesting to the widely held belief of descent from the Tribe of Dan, one of the Lost Tribes of Israel.

The challenge to Rabbi Hadane: How to teach Talmud-based (Orthodox) Judaism and preserve the basics of the old, Ethiopian-Jewish traditions.

Studying to be a rabbi in Israel

Special People ...who bring special interests and talents to Israel

This young man has chosen a different direction—the old way.

He is following in the footsteps of his fathers, and hopes to become a *qes*—a priest and Rabbi combined.

His studies also include codes and Talmud in the Orthodox tradition.

Kol Yisrael, Israel Radio, broadcasts a nightly
program in the Amharic language of general news
and special features.

Quality work
portrays life in Ethiopia and
receives acclaim in Israel.

Many see a touch of humor and social comment
in this work. Here, the man kindly helps the woman
secure the heavy water jug so she can carry it from
the river to home or market. A real gentleman.

Sculptors and their Work

Street Podiatrist
A not uncommon scene in Ethiopia

Ethiopian sculpture elicits interest at Jerusalem Convention.

A Student Artist In Israel

Who can measure the ways of the human spirit? To have gone through the personal turmoil, danger, and suffering in Ethiopia and to come out wanting to be an artist, to draw and to inspire… says much of the courage of the Beta Yisrael.

Ethiopian Immigrants Dance Ensemble performs at The Museum of the Diaspora at Tel Aviv University.

"The Hunt"... Association of Ethiopian Immigrants dancers and musicians hold audience enthralled at Bar Ilan University with the beat and tension of a leopard hunt.

ISRAEL DEFENSE FORCES
The Best School for Immigrants

Raised in a tradition of respect for authority, the Beta Yisrael are making a good record in the Army.

Several have qualified for the top-rated Paratroop Brigade and completed the grueling final tests of forced marching and endurance.

The entire nation watched in admiration as TV showed them reaching the final goal at the Western Wall, smiling and undaunted.

Receiving the Purple Beret on conclusion of strenuous basic training and initiation into the prestigious Givati Brigade.

First Ethiopian girl to complete the Army Officers' Course.

Learning the national pastime at Or Akiva.
Every open space becomes a soccer field.

Centuries of walking and running in mountainous terrain, plowing fields, bringing in harvest or fighting drought, chasing or running away from animals or marauders—small wonder that the Beta Yisrael have the build and talent for excellence in sports. Some will reach the status of professional athletes which invariably hastens the process of full integration for all.

A sunny spring day, and vocational school students from all over the country gather in Tel Aviv's Sportek for a day of competitive sports.

A highlight—this tug of war between two school teams. The scene becomes more than ordinary when you consider that these muscular fellows were no more than skin and bones when Operation Moses whisked them to Israel, three years before this photo was taken.

100

Olympic Hopeful

This beautiful immigrant of 28 (studying to be a nurse now) walked two hungry, danger-filled weeks with an infant in a back sack from a humble village to the Sudanese border. For two nights she hid in a hut. Her first 6 weeks of "absorption" into Israel were spent at her baby's side in a hospital as he slowly was cured of all of Job's plagues, inside and out. Inbal's luminous eyes evoke tears as she relates her story.

"My father was a weaver over there. Actually, he still is. Everyone said his cloth was the whitest, the softest, the best. Do they need weavers in Israel?"

"It will come…
It will come…
It will come…
Even the Messiah will come…
So why not my letter?"

The tug of war, the runner, waiting for a letter—all are paradigm for the challenges of the new life and lend a new meaning to the *Time of Fire*—different dangers and unfamiliar pitfalls.

The handicaps of language and unequal schooling; having a different view of Jews and Judaism and confusion of loyalty to traditions against other ways here, and confusion at finding a largely secular society in the Holy Land; how much of our culture can we cling to?… practical problems—choices of trade or career, studies, places to live and work; not enough pocket money or busfare (so important for those with strong family feelings); pressures from neighbors, superiors and officials who are not always patient and do not always understand (though many try); bad memories and poor communications that hamper the development of new friendships and trust; and above and through it all, a feeling of being alone—especially if mother or father or a beloved family member is still back there.

If young people get through all this and to the next stage in life, they can *bench gomel* (Hebrew prayers on escaping from danger), or thank the powers that be in the subtle and terse way of the Amharic, thank them that

meqseft yasferawal
"a catastrophe didn't happen!"

כי היכי דשתלו לי אבהתי
אנא נמי אשתיל לבראי

As my ancestors planted for me, so shall I plant for those who come after me.

Talmud, Taani

Planting trees in Soldiers Forest

1986

The Family

ቤተ ፡ ሰብ

beta sab

He who is without a wife...
dwells without blessing —
And without defence
against temptation.
Talmud, Yevamot, 62b

Woman without man
is like a field without seed.
Ethiopian Proverb

A second look at the quotes above reveals that in essence the Talmud says a man shouldn't be without a wife, while the Ethiopian proverb teaches that a woman shouldn't be without a husband. The difference in emphasis is not to be ignored.

Ethiopian culture requires the woman to honor the man, yet the Beta Yisrael wife had a higher degree of equality in some ways than her counterpart in a traditional old-country Jewish home as we knew it. True, the *balabbat* (the Amharic word is cognate to the Hebrew "master of the house") never set foot in the kitchen, but the wife was not excluded from the living room and could express an opinion in the presence of any visitors. Nor was she placed out of sight in the synagogue. More strikingly, she could circumcise an infant, part of her function as the chief tender of the woman in the *yaras gojo*, the birthing hut.

In Jewish households of all cultures, the major decisions were made by father, undoubtedly the common heritage of the Biblical, patriarchal model. Still, the Beta Yisrael woman made women's lib noises in producing goods and selling it at the market, though this was undoubtedly a latter day necessity.

In the old days, too, family life centered around the *tukul* or *gojo*, and the organization of what went on in and around that was largely in the hands of the woman. The round, thatched hut served as home and hearth, cooking place, and dining and sleeping place for family, for an endless stream of visitors and, sometimes, for the animals.

The extensive yard around the dwelling was an integral part of the home and the ambience was that of a busy workshop. Grain was stored in and around the huts in bins of dried mud or clay containers, and as long as they were filled, there was a feeling of security and even of plenty. If there was enough *tef* (a grain similar to millet and highly nourishing, apparently not grown outside of Ethiopia), then there would be enough *injera*—the puffy, absorbent roundbread that was the staff of life.

A weaver's loom might be anchored to a hole in the ground in the yard and not far from it the smithy is busy tinkering, mending and working iron into useful utensils as a boy pumps the bellows. Grain is being stone-ground and baskets are woven from special grass into many useful objects, from small, decorative items to large containers and flat tables. Elsewhere, clay and soil are mixed and shaped, and cups, pitchers and other ceramic items are dried and baked for use at home or for sale at market.

A visitor to the village probably would not notice that there was no special play area set aside for the children nor any equipment for their amusement. This is because the children were a natural part of the work, fetch, carry, helping picture. Actually, there *was* a playground waiting for them when they were at leisure, and it was just at hand beyond the village. The hills, the trees, the bushes, the stones, the sticks and the animals themselves—all were waiting for little hands, all were fun.

A few round huts with cone-shaped roofs—some secured at the top by a decorative ceramic nub—might be set within an enclosure, forming an extended family where a son has established a new household with his wife and children. Several of these enclosures would comprise a tightly knit, mutually supporting Beta Yisrael village... though the neighbors would call it a Falasha village derisively.

The woman's role in regulating family life began with her function as mate and bearer of children for which the Torah had set the rules almost 3500 years ago.

> *And if a woman have an issue of blood... seven days she*
> *shall be in her menstruation and every one who touches her shall*
> *be unclean until evening and... shall wash his clothes and bathe*
> *himself in water...*

Leviticus 15:19-22

Choosing measures that were more stringent than any followed by any Jewish community in history, the Beta Yisrael simply removed the menstruating woman out of the family circle and into a separate hut. This practice may also have been followed by the Qemant branch of the Agua tribe. (The extent to which the Agua adopted Judaism and the mixture of the Jews with some of the over seventy Ethiopian ethnic groupings is a matter of much unresolved speculation and is discussed in detail in most of the works in the bibliography provided.)

The separation was especially trying for the girl who had just reached puberty, and yet it gave her identity and status. The Beta Yisrael were especially supportive of the segregated woman, for was she not fulfilling a *mitzvah* (commandment) of the Torah?

The internal organization—economy and feeding functions—was totally geared to this predictable absence of a part of the family work force. The society could afford these absences and fit them easily to its patterns. Strangely, a parallel arrangement occurs in Israel today with the army reserves, where men regularly— though with less predictability as to timing—are taken away from their work and families for periods of service in the citizen's army. Law requires them to receive their compensations, even as did the women in the Ethiopian Jewish village.

In the *yadam gojo*, the hut of blood, the woman is cared for and food is passed over the wall or circle of stones around the hut without touching her. The hut is a flimsy, lean-to affair, though leaves and straw are thick enough and the roof so slanty as to make it liveable during the rains. As the twilight hour comes on the seventh day, the woman bathes herself, washes her clothes and, to display special piety, might also shave her head and, with the darkness, returns home, quite close by.

When the woman is ready to give birth, she also enters this hut, but now with two assistants. At birth these midwives emit twelve shouts of joy for a boy and nine for a girl, clearly broadcasting the news to the village which has been tuned in and listening.

Meanwhile, the family has been busy building the birthing hut, *yaras gojo*. The circumcision, a private affair, takes place on the eighth day (Genesis 17:12 and 21:4) in the old hut. Then, mother washes and moves to the new hut, where she remains for 32 more days for a total of forty for a baby boy; but if it was a girl, she remains in the first hut for a total of fourteen days, then moves to the "hut of women with infants" for 66 more days, completing 80 days all told. Haphazard? Not at all, it's all precisely as prescribed in Leviticus 12:2-5.

It is then, on the 40th or 80th day, that mother, child and all their clothing are again immersed—for the purpose of purification, it is carefully pointed out and not for entering the covenant, for that would be a kind of baptism. Only then do celebrations and namings take place, with equal joy for boy and girl, and equal blessings from the *Arde'et*, "The Falasha Book of the Disciples." The birthing shelter itself, being impure, is then burned.

The blessings are recited during bathing and purification. They are also inscribed delicately on parchment strips and carried or worn like a talisman. The magical quality of the amulet is underpinned with the surprising psychological insight that the efficacy of prayer lies in believing it, and that she is indeed blessed who acts as if she were.

> *Happy are they who read this prayer...*
> *Happy are they who believe in the words of this prayer...*
> *A blessing will come upon their homes and children.*
> *The angels will never be far from them...*
> *And you—if you have believed in this prayer—*
> *Your every wish will be granted.*
>
> (Wurmbrand, *Arde'et*, p. 59)

If the prayers helped, so did the period of isolation which can certainly be viewed as salutory for recuperation. It also gave the infant a chance to gain strength and protected it against the many diseases around. Burning the house would seem a good sanitary measure by any standard. Given such health care and inner spiritual strengths, Beta Yisrael should have numbered many times the estimated 250,000 when rediscovered over a century ago. But the ravages of man and nature had willed it otherwise. After that, the disintegration process speeded up considerably till there were no more than some 30,000 left in the 1970s when migration to Israel began to pick up momentum. Most of these were still leading the same rural existence as their fathers.

Whether the village ways are viewed as a simple, idyllic farm life, or a hard life of drudgery and striving to survive at a subsistence level, the vastly different realities of life that faced the Beta Yisrael at the end of their journey to the Promised Land became evident at once. The culture shock must have been tremendous, far beyond the ability of those who experienced it to verbalize and far deeper than those who tried to observe and measure it could probe.

Routine was gone and all the functions and clear-cut identities of the family members were jumbled. How can you duplicate all this in a hostel, hotel, or apartment building and in a different language with new, strange people all about? It wasn't a question of whether life was easier or its quality upgraded (and the latter is open to challenge)—just that it was vastly different.

Nor was it that the immigrants were suddenly faced with strange, new gadgets. Many weren't entirely unknown to them. Those who had lived in Gondar City and in Addis knew all about autos, electricity, radios, and faucets. Even the villagers had seen a car or a bus and observed a plane in overflight. It was the differences in the society and its people that seemed unbridgeable.

For many, most shattering was the blow to their religious expectations. Through the work of Jacques Faitlovitch, his predecessors and followers, the existence of the Jews of the rest of the world had long been known. Visitors had inspired brass candelabra for the synagogues. Star of David motifs appeared everywhere, on women's dresses and on the roofs of the *mesgid* (synagogue). Hebrew prayers and songs had been introduced by the teachers from Israel. All these were only symbols and gave little hint of the real state of religious observance in Israel.

It was most difficult for mother. The absence of a few central requirements threatened to shatter family life as she had known it, perhaps beyond repair.

First and foremost was the lack of the menstruation hut. It would have been a comparatively simple matter to set aside a small building near the absorption centers or even an apartment within one. Better would have been to send women without their children for a week to a rest center, such as the ones run by the women of WIZO in Herzlia for mothers with many children or Naamat for working women. Once such a significant religious practice was dispensed with by simply not providing for it, the fabric of the old ways began to come apart and it wasn't hard to look around and see that the average Israeli didn't care about all that.

There was another, less dramatic, but painful lesson. On arriving in Israel, it was very difficult to make *injera*. True, there was no *tef* but barley was used "at home" too, and here it came all ground up in packages. The stove provided hardly the right kind of fire, but adjustments would be made to that as well. But what could you substitute for the flat, ceramic pan, the *megogo* on which to bake the bread? It took weeks till the urgency of supplying large enough pans was realized. In this, as in much else, adaptability and patience slowly brought order back to family life. Gradually mother found that she *could* pass on the household and crafts culture to her daughter.

Though the exact spices for making *wat* were not available, one could substitute. It is remarkable to see how many ways and habits remain basically unchanged. Eating is one of them. The Beta Yisrael, at least during the first period after their arrival, ate little here because they ate little at home. Often, there wasn't much and sometimes almost nothing. A slight build and shrunken stomach combine to suppress appetite. They travel hours in Israel to a public meeting, listen to speeches for hours and travel home... and taste almost nothing all day without complaint.

A daily diet in Gondar consists of *bunna* and shared pieces of sliced fruit, and bread and milk for the children for breakfast. Lunch may be two, at the most three *injeras* dipped in *wat*—a spicy stew—which the porous *injera* sops up, eaten by hand entirely without utensils. *Doro wat* is the Ethiopian national dish, made with tender chicken simmered in berbere sauce, and is served with an endless stack of *injera*.

These descriptions of the village and its people encompass the majority of Beta Yisrael, but not all. A considerable number live in the capital city, Addis Abeba (New Flower), founded in 1885 by Emperor Menelik II, featuring Africa Hall, museums, modern structures and avenues, and excellent climate and high altitude. Some Beta Yisrael youth from there quickly became leaders of the community in Israel, having arrived with a post-high school education and greater sophistication than their country cousins.

A young woman from Addis, now on her way to a university degree, wrote an essay in an English improvement class right after her arrival. Presented as she wrote it, it reveals the level of English she had achieved there, but also demonstrates the deep feeling for mother and family that remains the hallmark of Beta Yisrael of any background.

> *My Mother, My mother's name is _____. She is a house wife. She is very responsible and she worked very hard. Because she is the mother of 9 children. She cooked the food for all families so she tried. Also she was sick when she got pregnancy. And she has responsibility for every child go to school, clean the clothes and she was very worried for the children when they sick even if when they late to come back home or for lunch.*

The children weren't the only ones to lean on mother, as witness this Ethiopian proverb—

> *If a friend hurts you... run to your wife!*

Family ties—within Israel and between Israel and Ethiopia—remain a powerful factor in life—most supportive if someone of the family is nearby, and most painful if fate, national pride and unfeeling hearts keep family members apart. At least letters generally get through and sometimes, even a phone call.

The following letter from a mother in Ethiopia had to reach its destination in Israel before she had any chance of talking to her son whose voice she had not heard since their separation three years earlier.

My son,

On Monday, August 10, from noon to 2 p.m. (the hours in the letter are different, as 6 a.m. is zero hour in Ethiopia, not midnight) *I will be at* (name and phone number of an acquaintance in Gondar city). *This gives you 4 weeks to get this letter and make arrangements to use a telephone. Do not fail to call me. I have to walk over four hours from the village, and it will take me five hours to get back, because of the hill. I have no place to sleep in Gondar.*

All my troubles will be like half if I can hear your voice. Temattena (I plead with you).

Ennat (mother)

It is a tiny footnote to history, that the 50 year-old mother made the nine hour round-trip walk, reached the phone on time and the call was actually completed!

It would be hard to emulate this act of devotion in Israel today. Instead of the footpaths that link the hamlets in Gondar, roads and buses to every corner of the country tie Beta Yisrael families to each other here.

Yet the same urge to be with the family persists. People go to great lengths to be together, including long walks through city streets when public transportation stops for Jewish holidays.

Bed and food are shared with relatives as a matter of course. Money is often shared when it is lacking. Families may pool resources for one household to buy furniture; then, when it is repaid to the pool, it is passed on to the next household for a television set. Clothing may be passed on and care of infants provided as needed. A cousin may be ill or a student short a textbook. Someone always needs some special help.

When there is an emergency in Ethiopia, money is collected and sent. The plowing ox may have died or the goat stolen, crises of potentially disastrous consequences.

In the morning the women gather, in the evening the men. The house is filled with endless talk, free-flowing, strong and open. There is much smiling and laughter, and an outsider is surprised and skeptical when a translator recounts the serious matters being discussed.

Children sit quietly in the family circle, and it is a beautiful sight to see a young person rise in respect, naturally and graciously, for a parent or relative. A special handshake emphasizes this diffidence, as the young person gives support to his outstreched arm by grasping his forearm with his left hand. He is thus holding back, intruding less into the space of his elder. If the person is old or very honored, the youth will bow toward his knees, recalling the days when the knees were actually kissed as a sign of subjection.

Gestures such as these, and the common greeting of multiple and mutual kissing on alternate cheeks that increase in number with the length of separation, are heart-warming testimony to the depth of family feeling and the caress of gentility that enveloped the ways and traditions of the Beta Yisrael. Though similar forms are found elsewhere in Africa, the influence of biblical teachings can somehow be discerned in all the ways of this Torah-trained House of Israel. Surely the gentle children have heeded the advice of Solomon, the wise—

Hear, my son, the instruction of thy father,
And forsake not the teaching of thy mother.

Proverbs 1:8

Nothing brings back the feeling of family closeness in a Jewish way as does the *sanbat*. The Sabbath Queen who once brought blessing, still makes her presence felt midst the family in Israel. The Sabbath in the village remains the sharpest of all memories, and a simple question to a well-settled professional man called forth many nostalgic recollections, served up with the freshness of the special Sabbath bread he so lovingly describes.

> *On Friday afternoon, my father would measure his shadow out in the field. When it was twelve footsteps long, he would announce that the sanbat has arrived. Everyone put down his work and went home.*
>
> *Mother prepared, in honor of the sanbat, a seasoned loaf that is called barakete, like brakha, 'blessing' in Hebrew. It was mother's responsibility to be careful that the grain lasted through the season, because everything there goes according to the rain and the seasons. For the sanbat she always seemed to manage.*
>
> *Sanbat morning the whole family takes that bread to the qesoch in the synagogue. (They are not necessarily from a priestly family. Anyone who studies long and hard enough can become a kohen or a qes.) Now the high priest of all the qesoch blesses the bread of each household, he cuts and distributes it to everybody, because it has now become communal bread. He gives to the qesoch first, then to the elders, then to the men and then to women, up to the smallest child. Then everyone eats and drinks talla, a kind of home-brewed beer.*
>
> *Everyone listens to the prayers and the reading from the Orit. And the elders tell all kinds of stories.*
>
> *Now all day, no one can leave the village. And, of course, no kind of work can be done. Maybe it sounds strict, but it wasn't. There was just time, plenty time. That was the day just to be a family. To feel very close. Then the stars came out, and the sanbat was over.*
>
> *Many things are not the same here. Many things have changed. Sanbat, though we call it here Shabbat, still feels like sanbat. That is because the family comes together on that day, and the love for each other remains unchanged.*

Three verses from the Torah epitomize the beauty of holiness that hovered over traditional family life and reached its climax every Sabbath.

כבד את־אביך ואת־אמך כאשר צוך יהוה
למען יאריכן ימיך ולמען ייטב לך
על־האדמה אשר־יהוה אלהיך נתן לך:

Honor thy father and thy mother
That thy days may be long,
And that it may go well with thee
Upon the land which the Lord thy G-d giveth thee.

The Fourth Commandment...
Deuteronomy 5:16

ויברך אלהים את־יום השביעי ויקדש אתו
כי בו שבת מכל־מלאכתו

And G-d blessed the seventh day and hallowed it
Because He rested thereon from all His work...

Genesis 2:3

מה טבו אהליך יעקב,
משכנתיך ישראל.

How goodly are your tents, O Jacob,
Your dwelling places, O Israel.

Numbers 24:5

Some Are at Home

Some Are Still in Temporary Housing

Sons Reunited with Fathers

Reunion on the Holy Day of *Sigd* in the hills of Jerusalem. Honoring grandmother with many kisses, much love, and total respect.

The longer it has been since you have seen someone of your family, the more cheek to cheek kisses you exchange.

Families gather at the Western Wall of the Mount where the biblical Temple of Solomon stood. This place symbolized Jerusalem, the focus of Beta Yisrael longing and prayers for centuries.

"They say I look like my mother. G-d, if I only had her strength... and that of the generations behind her..."

Separated for two decades, the son is a veteran in Israel and mother came with Operation Moses.

At the Academy Library, Boys Town, Jerusalem. A mother's pride as she brings her son to the halls of learning.

A leading *qes* brings his son to the *Sigd* in Jerusalem, November 1987.

Mother and son share an experience.

Happiness
Sisters are Reunited
June 1987

Newcomers

December, 1984 — Operation Moses

First day —
Off the plane. Night in Ashkelon in a luxurious cottage near the sea. "Is this what Israel is like?"

Second day —
Clothing. Briefing. Registering. "Where is my uncle?"

Third day —
To Givat Olga, also near the sea... but the two tall buildings are on the wrong side of the tracks.
"Much colder here than it ever gets in Gondar."
"Quiet after all the excitement."
"We are home. Baby seems to like it."

Veterans in The Land

Brother... Brother... Sister

The staircase —
    and our lives —
        go only up!

One family, three generations, now finally together in Israel.

A Healing Family

Father is a male nurse at a leading hospital and is active in the Beta Yisrael community. Mother is studying nursing. Family began in the city of Lod and has now moved to a larger apartment in Jerusalem.

A further sign of "modernity"—there are only two children in this family, a rarity among Beta Yisrael, where four to ten children are usual.

Mother will graduate accounting course in mid-1988. She eagerly looks forward to begin working now that the girls are old enough... and, happily, their grandparents are here now to help.

Father is the 1987 Gold Medal Winner as Outstanding Worker of the Year at Israel Aircraft Industries. Though his own parents have already arrived, he continues his activity as a member of the National Rescue Committee to finish the Exodus for all Ethiopian Jews.

Bright and popular with their Israeli friends, the two girls are, by all accounts, the crowning success of a happy family.

Young Families in Israel
Challenge and Upward Mobility

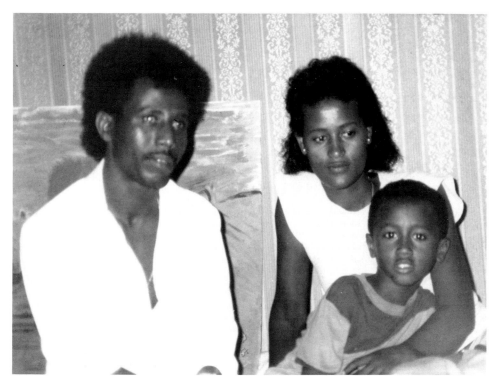

Mother is a dental assistant. Father works in a factory... and is also an artist, plays the *krar*, a lyre he fashioned himself.

"Your son is a pleasure," reports teacher — and parents couldn't agree more.

Father is one of the bright young men who works as counselor/social worker with the Beta Yisrael families.

After finishing special studies and training with the Ministry of Absorption, father considers himself doubly blessed that he can help the Beta Yisrael in the Central Region face the many challenges he met when he was a new immigrant just a few years ago.

There are three partners in the creation of every child... father, mother and G-d.

The Zohar

Nazareth. A strange place for the first home of a Beta Yisrael family. Still, the hills feel familiar.

Mother, a student. Father, a student. Children likewise. Family is in the country long enough so that most of their relatives are here.

Brother and Sister — Citizens of Beauty and Dignity.

Shalom

A peaceful life at last

הגיד לך אדם
מה טוב;
ומה ה';
דורש ממך
כי אם עשות
משפט
ואהבת חסד
והצנע לכת
עם-אלהיך.

מיכה ו:ח

"It hath been told
thee, O man, what
is good. And what
the Lord doth
require of thee;
Only to do justly,
and to love
mercy, and to
walk humbly with
thy God."

Micah 6:8

Sanctification in Life

ሰንበት

sanbat

*More than the Jews
preserved the Sabbath,
did the Sabbath preserve the Jews.*
Ahad Ha'Am

*The savior of the Jews
is the Sabbath.*
Saying of the Ethiopian Jews

Awareness of a Jewish community in Ethiopia was still scant in the 1960's even amongst rabbis and Jewish organizations. Something interesting was going on there. There were black Jews, living some sort of tribal life in the mountains and somehow managing to hold on to some Jewish tradition.

None but a few anthropologists and some Christian missionaries could even begin to guess at the fullness of Jewish life in the Beta Yisrael villages. The Torah was read and treasured, *kashrut* was observed, religious weddings were performed, and boys were circumcised.

Life here was vastly different from the rest of the Jewish world, so it was natural that there were differences in understanding the Torah and differences in practice. Farmers emphasized simpler values related to their lives. Torah laws concerning domesticated animals were observed with total understanding:

"Thou shalt not muzzle an ox while he is threshing" (Deuteronomy 25:4). Of course, working oxen in a grain field and preventing them from eating a bit of grain is cruelty.

"Thou shalt not boil a kid in its mother's milk" (Exodus 23:19). Obviously, a barbaric practice. The prohibition was extended to cooking any meat in milk.

Kill an animal only for food; and only if it is *kosher* as defined in Leviticus, Chapter 11; and only after its blood has been drained and covered (Leviticus 17:13); and only with care and prayer, including a recital of the Ten Commandments.

The First Commandment begins: *"I am the Lord... who brought thee out of the land of Egypt, out of the house of bondage"* (Exodus 20:2). The same words are used in Leviticus 11:25 to provide a "reason" or moral basis for the idea of kosher food—*"For I am the Lord that brought you up out of the land of Egypt... ye shall therefore be holy..."* No people can be free or holy if it practices cruelty to man or beast.

The rabbis believed that eating *kosher* food and observing the Sabbath were the two pillars of Jewish survival. It was clearly so in the Ethiopian pale of Jewish settlement where belief was firm in *Egzi'abeher Amlaka Israel*, the Lord, G-d of Israel. His laws were in the *Orit*, the precious teachings of Moses, a guide for living as preserved in the ancient *Ge'ez*, the language of Torah and prayer. The *Orit* included all the holy writings and was kept in a square chamber in the middle of the synagogue, the Holy of Holies, where only the *qesoch*, or *kahenat*, entered.

The community gathers on Sabbath and holy days and the *qesoch* lead prayers with the help of their assistants and chanters, the *dabtara*, much like the Levites in the *Beit Hamikdash* in ancient Jerusalem: *"May G-d alone be exalted in justice and right. There is no other G-d!"*

...and the people answer, *"Amen."*

"Behold, like the Children of Cush, you are unto Me, the Children of Israel!
Amos 9:7

...and the people answer *"Jerusalem, Jerusalem."*

The major festivals are all celebrated by the Beta Yisrael in accord with the dates and ways of observance described in the Torah. The variances in observance from the rest of the Jewish world occur where the Torah is not specific or clear or its meaning is open to interpretations. Rabbinic Judaism interpreted the Torah in its fashion and through its rules and so did the Beta Yisrael, though in a much simpler way and following scriptures literally.

The rabbis, additionally, had the faith to declare that their dicta was inherent in the law given to Moses and therefore was of equal validity with the written Torah. The rabbis, therefore, were obliged to examine every open question and created the Oral Law, codified chiefly in the Babylonian Talmud, while the early Beta Yisrael produced a literature that dealt with the belief in G-d, the necessity of following the commandments, the angels who served G-d and helped or hindered man in his efforts to follow the way of the Torah, the rewards that awaited the pious in heaven and the punishments for the others in hell. Their writings are based on the Torah and on the Book of Jubilees and other apocryphal books, that is, those that were not considered sufficiently authentic for inclusion in the Bible.

For the Beta Yisrael, the biblically ordained year began with *Fasika, Pesach* in Hebrew, the Feast of Passover. The vernal festival was celebrated as the rites of spring by many peoples, but the rebirth of nature was eclipsed by the birth of the

People as the theme of Passover, when the liberated slaves left Egypt in a hurry on their way to Sinai and the Torah, then finally to the Land beloved of their fathers.

Thus, with the moon at its fullest, the 15th of *Lissan* (*Nissan* in Hebrew) marks the first of the seven days of *Fasika* when *kitta* (*matzah*) is eaten. The Paschal lamb is sacrificed (the only offering still observed of all those ordained in the Torah) and consumed on the eve of the fourteenth. An all night vigil follows, but the ceremonial meal called the *seder* is not conducted the way the rabbis later evolved it out of the biblical verses. Exodus 13:8 commands that *"you shall tell your son,"* and that the *qes* certainly does, and with increased fervor now that the original Exodus story has become the hope and the symbol for the new Exodus that awaits completion.

The next of the three Pilgrim Festivals is the Feast of Weeks, *ma'rar*, a harvest festival when a communal feast is shared in the synagogue. Again a divergence. The Torah says (Leviticus 23:15) *"Count off, after the rest day... seven full weeks."* The rabbis decided that "the rest day" was the first day of Passover, but the Beta Yisrael decided that as the last day of Passover was also a "rest day" it is logical to begin counting for the next holiday when this one is all over. So The Feast of Weeks occurs on the sixth day of the third month, but the Beta Yisrael *ma'rar* begins on the twelfth. As it is not reaping season in Ethiopia then, another harvest festival is celebrated six months later when the grain is ripe.

The third of the festivals when the people walked up to Jerusalem, is the Feast of Booths. Here the dates agree, beginning on the 15th of the seventh month (time of the harvest moon in the western world). *"So that your* (future) *generations will know that I made the Children of Israel live in booths when I brought them out of the land of Egypt"* (Leviticus 23:43).

A booth is a shack made of cut branches, leaves, fronds, rushes and the like. Could the hut of the Beta Yisrael, the *tukul*, be considered a booth? Of course, that's exactly what it was... and for that reason the Beta Yisrael formerly did not build booths for the Feast of Tabernacles—they already lived in them.

It wasn't so rare throughout Jewish history for the Children of Israel to find themselves living in flimsy shacks, exposed to cold winds and the evil intentions of their tormentors.

October, 1946—Jewish Chaplains with the US Army visit Babenhausen in the American zone of Germany where survivors of the Holocaust have been given temporary shelter for processing and distribution among the more established displaced persons camps. Thousands have been filling the prefab huts spread over a huge area.

The first thing the commanding officer requests is that the chaplains find out why the Jews are building little huts next to each of the big huts? He has no common language with them, and they are creating quite a disorder, cutting branches and scrounging lumber. "I don't have to ask," says the chaplain, deeply moved by the sight of his homeless brothers fulfilling the Torah commandment. "It's the Feast of Tabernacles."

He wondered, though, if they were required to build them, as they were already in temporary dwellings. That was the key difference that may have rendered the *tukul* unqualified as a booth. It was a permanent dwelling. It kept out wind and rain quite well. The refugees in Germany would go on to cross mountains and oceans "illegally" in their push against the might of the British army and navy. They would be imprisoned on Cyprus for many months, yet in the end complete their Exodus to the State of Israel. There they would fight in the battle for independence, build homes and reconstruct their lives.

135

For the Beta Yisrael the *tukul* had been home, apparently unchanged, for centuries. The time was long overdue to move them into more substantial, safer dwellings where they would "*sit every man under his vine and under his fig tree, and none shall make them afraid*" (Micah 4:4).

New Year and the Day of Atonement are observed on the Torah dates, the first and the tenth of the seventh month. The New Year Holy Day is called "The Light (apparently of Abraham) is Rising." The Binding of Isaac is recalled, as it is in the western Torah reading. No specific instrument is specified in the Torah for sounding *truah* on the New Year (Leviticus 23:24), so the Beta Yisrael sound the cymbals, probably because Psalm 150 attaches the word *truah* to cymbals. The rabbis didn't know what to blow either, but accepted a tradition that a *shofar*, a ram's horn, is used—to recall the ram sacrificed in place of Isaac.

Yom Kippur encompasses a night and a day of contrition and prayer. *Astasreyo* — the Day of Atonement is the most serious of all the fast days, of which there are several, including the Ninth of Ab marking the destruction of the Temple and a weekly Thursday fast.

The day ends with the *emen* ceremony, the spreading of grain for the birds, commemorating the dead. As the birds eat the seed, the prayers are seen as being accepted. Food and drink has been prepared for a communal breaking of the fast and the long and happy celebration contrasts sharply with the somberness of the day. The blessings, kissing, and embracing has a parallel in the well-known Yemenite exuberance on Yom Kippur night, even to the partying found today in western synagogues. The joy of feeling cleansed and forgiven harks back to ancient Jerusalem when the High Priest came out of the Holy of Holies on Yom Kippur and the scarlet fillet had turned white as a sign that the people had been forgiven. A night of great festivity followed that included selection of brides and announcement of betrothals.

The New Moon is a full festival day (Numbers 28:11-15) and to find it observed as a semi-festival, working day in Israel dismayed The Beta Yisrael. They, themselves, have added a series of unique, mnemonic festivals that occur every month whose function it is to keep the major festivals fresh and meaningful all through the year. These are the Festival of the Tenth (to remember the Day of Atonement which occurs on the tenth of the seventh month), the Festival of the Twelfth (for the Feast of Weeks), and the Festival of the Fifteenth (for Passover and Tabernacles).

Of the minor festivals, Purim is observed only as the Fast of Esther for three days, with food permitted at night. The general foolishness and rejoicing over the fall of Haman that characterizes the western tradition is hard for the *kahenat* (the priesthood) in Israel to accept. Gifts were always distributed to the poor however, as called for in the Book of Esther. With the poor comprising a solid majority in the villages today, one wonders what can be left of the custom.

Hardly any Jewish community anywhere, anytime, could match in piety the Sabbath observance in a Beta Yisrael village. Even the darkened streets of strictly orthodox Bnei Brak on a Friday night in Israel today can't match the dark of the village when the fires had burned down round the *tukuls*. Inside, beeswax candles might last till bedtime. In modern times, gas lamps are lit before sunset and left to burn out. All other stoves or fires are put out before Sabbath.

Sanbat thus means no fire for warmth or cooking, no labor, no travelling, no instruments at prayer, no quarrels and—contrary to rabbinic admonitions to "be fruitful and multiply" on Sabbath eve—no cohabitation.

Food is eaten cold on *Sanbat*, though not without joy and blessing—especially at the community meal in the synagogue.

> *Then the Sabbath will... say to her Creator: 'These are my people; these are my inheritance; these are they who walk in my path, who love me, who believe in me, who neglect Thee not, who find delight in Thee. Now they will enjoy eternal rest. Amen.*

Te'ezaza Sanbat (Leslau, *Falasha Anthology*, p. 38)

In the sacred literature of the Beta Yisrael, the *Te'ezaza Sanbat, The Commandments of the Sabbath*, is both allegory and a handbook of codes, in which the Sabbath is portrayed as a beautiful woman, present at creation.

Rabbi Shlomo Halevi Alkabez, a mystic of Safed, also pictured the Sabbath as a woman, a lovely bride. Indicative of contacts or common sources with Rabbinic Judaism, one of the long list of Sabbath prohibitions surprisingly parallels the talmudic wisdom that *"He who prepared on Friday, will eat on the Sabbath"* (Avoda Zara, 3b).

The *Te'ezaza Sanbat* is much harsher: "He who prepares not on Friday what he will eat, drink, or give (on the Sabbath)... shall die" (p. 20).

A Yiddish version was more realistic: "He who doesn't prepare on Friday, eats nothing on the morrow."

It was left to a cynical Israeli poet to top them all by commenting on the state of piety in Israel today ... and perhaps foretelling the future of some Beta Yisrael teenagers now observing the commandments in Orthodox schools.

"He who doesn't prepare on Friday, on Sabbath goes to the beach!"

A special sanctity is ascribed to every seventh Sabbath, a logical extension perhaps of every seventh day being holier than the others. The sanctity of the Sabbath was so strong, its effects lasted throughout the week. A Beta Yisrael phrase illustrates this, as well as the subtlety and usefulness of its sayings.

"Such a thing never happens on *sanbat*" is a protective phrase against misfortune all week long. This is the reasoning:

Suppose you were on your way to market (never on Shabbat of course, and since that is the chief market day, it helps explain why the Beta Yisrael never became traders or merchants) and wanted to allay a fear against monetary loss. Perhaps no one would buy the cloth you had woven, or someone would greatly underpay you for it, as often happened to the Jews, who, as Falashas, were easy prey to pressure and blackmail. You then might turn to your companion and say "Such a thing never happens on *sanbat*." Meaning:

1. Sabbath, being a day of rest, brings no aggravations.
2. (Extension) ...and especially in money matters am I protected, because I never engage in those on *sanbat*, so I certainly wouldn't be cheated on the price of this cloth on the *sanbat*.
3. (and here is the leap of hope over logic) ...and therefore it won't happen today either, though it isn't *sanbat!*

Perhaps it is faith and not only hope that overcomes the logic. "Since I am an observer of the Sabbath, would my protecting angel let a bad thing happen to me anytime?"

A more profound saying with roots in faith is "The Savior of the Jews is the *Sanbat.*"

Public disputations were the bane of the Jews of Europe in the Middle Ages. Rabbis were confronted with priests who challenged them to explain their rejection of Jesus. Death or the expulsion of a community could follow if the rabbis failed. If, however, the spokesman for the Jews could give a satisfactory answer which managed not to offend the Christians, though it neither accepted nor denied their Messiah, the community might be spared.

Such an answer was once given by the Beta Yisrael when pressed and tortured to name their savior. "The Savior of the Jews is the Sabbath!" they cried out. Of course, they meant it literally as the Sabbath was personified in their writings as their heavenly protector.

Western Jews had a similar phrase coined by Ahad Ha'am, a leading molder of modern Jewish culture. "More than the Jews preserved the Sabbath, did the Sabbath preserve the Jews." That is, it was the observance of the Sabbath which kept the Jewish people distinct and preserved their existence.

The remaining identifiable Beta Yisrael number over 30,000 today, divided between Israel and Ethiopia. That isn't saying much for the protecting Sabbath angel when we consider that they probably numbered over half a million at their zenith in ages past. Still, it is undeniable that this remnant owes its existence in large part to its tenacious loyalty to the Sabbath.

Will the Sabbath preserve the Beta Yisrael immigrants in Israel?

It didn't do so well with the first generation of immigrants to America. In fact, it may have been the demands of Sabbath observance that finished many of them as observant Jews. A job in America meant working on the Sabbath, and the dilemma was most commonly resolved in favor of giving up the Sabbath rather than your job. What could you do? You had to support your family. Once you "broke" the Sabbath, all other violations seemed minor and easy to fall into.

There were many other temptations or needs in America that led one away from the Sabbath, synagogue, and Jewish ways. With the "Americanization" of Israel, they exist here too. Though there is no work on the Sabbath and all shops are closed, the beach is open and mountains, forests, resorts, and friends and relatives in far away places are all temptations. Buses don't run, but the highways are clogged with cars, the newest vehicle for Sabbath violations. "Fortunately," very few Ethiopians can afford cars—as yet.

N.A. is a handsome, winning young man of about thirty. He hopes to finish his bookkeeping course in a year, and then he'll see about putting his life together again.

Does he, and the twelve Ethiopians living in a student hostel, ever go to the synagogue? Was religion part of his life when he was growing up in Ethiopia? Does he see a place for it in his future here?

"To understand my answer, I will have to tell you a little bit about my life," he began.

The basic outline of his story is similar to that of many Beta Yisrael here, but the similarities are overwhelmed by the particulars. His English required only moderate realignment.

"I am from Briyesus *mender* (village). We have been forty Jewish families, scattered around. We had no *mesgid* or *qes*, but there was one in Sanbatle, about ten kilometer away. There was *Qes* Menasse, but we did not go there for *sanbat*, only for holidays, like *Fasika*. Of course for the *Sigd* everyone went to Ambover about sixty kilometer away. There we had plenty of relatives and slept and ate with them... it was like socially being together."

"Now for *sanbat*, everyone just had it at home and the meal and everything... but sometimes people would gather in a home and have a worship service. My father was not a *qes*, but he must have studied because he knew the *Orit* and he would read from the Torah and he would also lead a service and people would say 'Amen,' like for a *qes*. And he taught me some Torah."

"I did not go to any Jewish school, but I know all the things to do and what not to do and about the holidays and *kasher* and all that. I know everything, because I was just doing it at home. Friday afternoon we would go down to the river, and I would wash my clothes with soap and then myself when I was seven years old, because we are twelve children and mother could not do it herself. The river was fast in places and I learn to swim, but many were afraid to swim."

"Now my father was a weaver, but also had sheep and goats. A man, not a Jewish man, would come to buy a sheep sometimes and became friends with my father... and he said would you like me to take one of your sons with me, so he could have an education and to live in our house? So that is how I was lucky to go to the Haile Selassie First Comprehensive School in Gondar and then the family moved to Addis Abeba and I went too. So I studied at the Ethio-American Institute, which was a private school."

"So now that family was not going to church at all and no one tried to make me a Christian, but very few people knew that I was a *Falasha*. Of course, we never eat any meat except at home, because it is not *kasher*... now when I am living with the family, I just did not think about that. They were like my family and whatever was there, I ate like everybody."

"Now here I do not go to the *Beit Knesset* (synagogue) because my Israeli friends don't go, and also it is not like a *mesgid,* and the *qes* does not lead the prayers. And besides, the religious, they all smoke (not on the *Sabbath*), and I am believing with my whole body in G-d and not just the outside; and G-d looks deep into the internal parts of the being and the smoking spoils the internal. So it is forbidden by the Jewish religion to smoke." (Today, the rabbis agree, even those who smoke.)

"Now there is also something, because two brothers and two sisters are here, and the rest of my family is there with my mother and father, who is now seventy-five. But also, I must say that I am married and also I have a son. And my wife and son, they are not here but far from me... and what can I do with all that first, before I think about questions if to go to the synagogue?"

So the question comes back to its askers. Can N. find solutions in a synagogue here... and one so different from the one he knew? His noting that the synagogue is not a *mesgid* is most telling. In truth, there is not one single *mesgid* in Israel where the *qesoch* chant the prayers in Ghe'ez, where the traditional instruments are heard and where there is a sharing of bread and a feeling of family. Ordinary rooms have been so used, however.

Is there a way to avoid paying so heavy a price for the comforts, freedoms and promises of Israel? Will the Beta Yisrael preserve its major traditions in Zion and Jerusalem, the fulfillment of ancient dreams? Has Israel made a promise, specific or implied, to help it do so?

Actually, on January 1, 1987, it did.

As *Hanukkah*, the Feast of Lights, approached in December 1986, the leadership of the Beta Yisrael made this appeal to the people and the Government of Israel:

THE SEVENTH CANDLE

An earnest message from the Ethiopian Jewish Community in Israel.

We, the Beta Yisrael, have long observed the Festivals of the Hebrew calendar; but only those that are biblically ordained. The one festival observed through the centuries by all Jews of the world except those of Ethiopia, is *Hanukkah*.

"In these days and at this season," the Festival of *Hanukkah* was passed on to us as a gift from the Jewish People and the State of Israel—a Festival of Light and inspiration that ties us, too, to those heroic days when the Lord gave "the many into the hands of the few."

By the light of the Seventh Candle, we ask confirmation of these Seven Promises inherent in the very existence of the State of Israel and its promulgation of the Law of Return, a welcoming beacon from Zion:

1. We will save you and preserve you.
2. We will redeem you and bring you all to your home in Israel.
3. We will take you to our hearts and fulfill the Torah verse *"And your brother shall dwell among you."*
4. We will help you find your way in your first years with us.
5. We will share with you the history and traditions of the Jewish People through the ages in many lands.
6. We will help you preserve your own traditions and memories.
7. We will open the way for you to equal opportunity for a life of productivity, freedom and light.

By the light of these candles, as we recall the heroism of the Maccabees, we also honor the memory of our own courageous people who perished crossing mountains and deserts on the way to the Land promised to Abraham, Isaac and Jacob, the Land of Israel.

The President of Israel endorsed the appeal. The President of the Knesset, Mr. Shlomo Hillel, invited the *qesoch* to a formal reception in Israel's parliament where they read the declaration, to which he added his own request on Israel Television "that in every home in Israel, the lighting of the Seventh Candle be dedicated to identification with the Jews of Ethiopia, just as we are accustomed to using the empty chair at Passover time to think about the Jews in the Soviet Union." *(Kol Yisrael*, December 29, 1986).

On January 1, 1987, as the seven candles were lit, the *qesoch* prayed in their hearts that Israel would fulfill all seven promises. They were grateful Israel had undertaken to complete Number 2—We will redeem you and bring you all to your home in Israel—but weren't sure if it would be achieved... or when. Neither the old *sanbat* or the "new" *Hanukkah* could keep their families in Ethiopia surviving—and surviving as Jews—much longer. And as for Number 6—We will help you preserve your own traditions and memories—it would indeed require a new miracle of *Hanukkah* for the flickering light of memory and tradition not to be extinguished and survive the unsettling period of the rededication of an ancient people in a new land.

שְׁמַע יִשְׂרָאֵל

Sh'ma Yisrael… Hear, O Israel, the Lord is our G-d, the Lord is One.

Bar Mitzvah for the Beta Yisrael is all new and not part of the Ethiopian Jewish heritage, there being no reference to it in Torah, nor was it practised by any Jews till at least the 13th Century. Yet it is an equalizer of sorts and allows the Ethiopian boys to feel equal status—in the Jewish religion, at least—with other boys of thirteen.

But how will the *qesoch,* the spiritual leaders of Beta Yisrael, influence them and be able to enrich their lives as they did back in the village of their origin?

These boys, observing their Bar Mitzvah at the Western Wall, have learned to read the *siddur* (prayer book), don *tallit* (prayer-shawl) and *tefillin* (phylacteries) and are well on their way to becoming loyal and observant Jews in Orthodox, Israeli style.

At an older age, the conflict of youth and tradition engulfs the Beta Yisrael. Arriving past high school age, these young men do not receive religious training in Israel.

In Ethiopia men wore no head covering as it is not required by Torah.

A few elders and *kahenat*, steeped in their own religious practices, are adding studies in rabbinic Judaism in the Meir Institute of Torah Studies in Jerusalem.

A talmudic dispute often brings smiles and good humor.

An Amharic copy of the Bible. "We could distribute hundreds of these here at once, if only someone would bring them from Ethiopia."

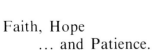

Faith, Hope
... and Patience.

The Wedding Ceremony

ሰርግ

sarg

According to Jewish tradition, matches are made in heaven, but in Ethiopia, as elsewhere, the earthly fathers make the arrangements. Betrothals can last several years and are made early to protect the girl from others while she is still living with her parents. A boy of eighteen and a girl of about thirteen are considered ready for marriage though most marriages take place when he reaches twenty and she sixteen.

The wedding formalities begin with an exchange of gifts. The families are blessed and commence celebrations, each in its own village. The bride's fingernails are dyed with henna, *esosela* in Amharic, used also by the Yemenite Jewish bride for beauty and as a protective charm. (Song of Songs 1:14.)

The groom's family moves to a specially constructed hut where the *keshera* or "tying" ceremony takes place. The *qes* carefully and publicly arranges two cords, then lifts them the length of the groom's body and ties them ceremoniously around his forehead. The white cord testifies that the groom is unsullied and the red is a symbol of the bride's virginity. With music and dancing, the groom's party then walks to the bride's village.

The bride's hut has also been specially built and there the ceremony is held. A certificate of marriage contains the specific terms agreed upon. A copy is given to each family and another is for the "registry," which in this case is the *qes*. Thus, it is similar to the rabbinic *ktubah*. Two witnesses sign and so do groom and bride, the latter at her own home. Fingerprints were the usual signature of bride and groom. The *qes* and a trustee acceptable to both sides also affix their signatures.

The bride is then brought ceremoniously to the wedding hut for blessing and parting from parents. Her parents are expected to cry without tears (sad that she's leaving, happy she's marrying), which takes some skill.

Wedding festivities go on for seven days (could they have known of the *sheva brachot*—the seven blessings of rabbinic Judaism?) and only after that do bride and groom enter their own home. Altogether, the wedding has lasted about ten days.

Many problems arise as the *qes* tries to incorporate all these huts and processions and other elements into a wedding in Israel today. It is easy though to add the rabbinic practices: holding a *huppah* or wedding canopy over the heads of the couple; using a printed orthodox marriage contract; completing the contractual nature of the ceremony by handing the groom the corner of a handkerchief, thereby acting out the agreement; using a plain gold band and having the groom place it on the index finger of her right hand while saying to the bride, "Behold, thou art sanctified unto me with this ring, according to the law of Moses and the Jewish people."

Some *qesoch* have learned to read the entire *ktubah*, a difficult task in the Aramic language of the Talmud. The groom even breaks the glass and everyone shouts *"Mazal Tov!"* in the Western manner.

Though there was strict monogamy and much devotion and loyalty within family life in Ethiopia, marriages there too sometimes fell apart. Poverty and other

The *qes* blessing the groom

The bride under the *huppah*

harsh conditions didn't help. Divorces were discouraged and there was much effort at reconciliation. The Passover week was a time for intensive counselling with parents, elders and the *qes*. Still, if all failed, a divorce was granted.

This, too, is a formal ceremony in which husband and wife dictate the terms to which they agree. These are incorporated in the writs of divorce they give each other. The date and place of divorce are noted, and the major document—the one given by the husband—is duly witnessed and signed by all, including the trustee who was at the wedding. It is all really very much like the Orthodox procedure, and no wonder. While no specific wedding ceremony is described in Torah there is a clear verse, Deuteronomy 24:3, which tells just how to divorce—*And he gives her a bill of divorcement.* It is this injunction that the Beta Yisrael now follow, and the divorce takes effect when the husband hands her the writ.

Investigators have described various other practices for the Beta Yisrael divorce, one saying the divorce consisted in tearing up of the wedding contract. Far more serious than the technicalities of divorce procedures are the terrible dislocations caused by the half-finished migration to Israel. This has resulted in a great deal of instability in the family structure that will take several generations and another miracle or two to heal.

The imagery of rabbinic Judaism has G-d Himself performing the wedding of Adam and Eve. Who else was there to do it? This idea is then extended to G-d as the only reliable matchmaker—and even He finds it hard to put the right people together. The talmudic adage puts it this way:

It is as difficult to arrange a suitable marriage as it was to divide the Red Sea!

Sota, 22

Perhaps the old saying holds out a hope. As He *did* divide the Red Sea, could He not reunite the Beta Yisrael couples split to both sides of it?

The photos shown on the following page were taken at a vocational, live-in school in Kfar Saba where two students were married. In place of building special huts and celebrating for days, various smaller buildings on the landscape grounds were used, and the seven days were compacted into seven hours.

Out of the groom's "hut" came the groom and his friends in festive procession, with singing and *eskesta* shoulder dancing accompanied by drum and *krar* (lyre) and made their way to the ceremonies and festivities held in the large auditorium of the school. With joy and love, principal, teachers and counselors helped and hosted, wined and dined, danced and gifted and were in every way *in loco parentis*. If ever a time and place in Israel approached the ambience of a mountain village in Gondar — that was it!

148

OLD WAY
Preparing the *keshera* cord
for the groom's brow

THE UNIVERSAL WAY
A beautiful bride

NEW WAY
Signing the *ktubah*,
Talmudic Marriage Contract

BOTH WAYS
Huppah (canopy)—Rabbinic
Ring on index finger—Rabbinic
keshera—Beta Yisrael
Music—Beta Yisrael

The Holy Day of The Sigd

የስግድ - ቀን

ye-sigd qan

The Revelation at Sinai

(Recited at the Sigd)

And the Lord called... out of the mountain, saying: ...Ye have seen what I did unto the Egyptians, and how I bore you on eagles' wings and brought you unto Myself (to Sinai). Now therefore, if ye will ... keep My covenant, then ye shall be Mine own treasure from among all peoples... (Exodus 19:3,4,5)

I am the Lord thy G-d, who brought thee out of the land of Egypt, out of the house of bondage. (First Commandment, Exodus 20:2)

And all the people perceived the thunder and the lightning and the sound of the shofar and the mountain smoking; and when the people saw it, they trembled and stood afar off. (Exodus 20:15)

አ

The *Sigd* is the most important festival of the Beta Yisrael. It is exclusively theirs. No other Jewish community celebrated it or even witnessed it until its reenactment in Israel on November 15, 1982, the 29th of *Heshvan* on the Hebrew calendar, forty-nine days after *Yom Kippur*. Only Beta Yisrael were permitted at the top of the hill in Ambover and at three other provincial centers.

The Beta Yisrael have put all their Jewish and personal feelings into this one day. Robed in dignity, an aura of purity and a spiritual élan hovering over the procession, they walk to the top of the hill to symbolize that they are leaving behind the land in which they have remained strangers; to show that they are drawing nearer to *Elohe, Malhe,* the Lord of Israel; to ascend the mountain and receive the Law, even as did their prophet Moses at Sinai; to face Jerusalem and look toward the land of Israel, even as did their father Abraham when the *"Lord appeared unto Abraham and said: 'Unto thy seed will I give this land'..."* (Genesis 12:7); to pray: *neu nesged,* "come and let us prostrate ourselves" and to bow before the King of Kings and lay their stones before Him as a sign of contrition and surrender (even as was the custom in front of a king of flesh and blood) and ask forgiveness from Him "whose heart is not vengeful, who purifies the unclean and blots out sins..." (Halévy, *Prieres de Falashes*).

They knew they were more sinned against than sinning. It was so hard to keep the laws of Moses in the threatening environment that pressured them and lured them, that looked upon them as sorcerers yet wanted their souls, that barred them from owning land, closed their schools and synagogues, scoffed at their ways, limited their livelihood, cheated them, imprisoned them and stole their sons away.

How comforting, then, to stand on top of the mountain and read the biblical words:

> *And the Children of Israel separated themselves from all strangers and confessed their sins... and said:...'Thou alone are the creator of heaven and earth... Thou art the Lord who chose Abraham... and found his heart faithful to Thee... and entered into a covenant with him... and his seed and Thou hast fulfilled Thy promise, for Thou art Righteous.'*
>
> Nehemia 9:2,3,7,8

These feelings and hopes reflect three major themes in the grand design of the Day of the *Sigd*, which can be viewed as a symbolic acting out of the major themes of Judaism itself.

First is the return to the land of Abraham, there to follow the *mitzvot* (the commandments)—even as the people did in the time of Ezra when many returned from the Babylonian exile.

The *qesoch* maintain that the first *Sigd* is described in the Bible in Nehemia, Chapters 8-10, which are accordingly read. As *they* returned in those days, so does Beta Yisrael long to return to Israel and worship in Jerusalem. The *qesoch* can point to the following verses in the Book of Nehemia and explain how the Beta Yisrael fulfilled them in the *Sigd:*

"And Ezra opened the book in the sight of all the people." (Chapter 8,5) — So do we gather the people and open the *Orit* for them.

"And all the people answered, 'Amen, Amen'... and they bowed their heads..." (8:6) — So do we, and we call the whole ceremony *The Day of the Sigd*, which in Amharic means "bowing"—as in *mesgid*, a synagogue or place of bowing. (The same root is used in Hebrew and Arabic.)

"...the Children of Israel were assembled with fasting..." (9:1)—So are we. Food and a feast are prepared the evening before, but are put aside, awaiting the end of the service and the fast.

"...they entered into an oath, to walk in G-d's law ... and to observe ... and do all the commandments." (10:30)—"and that we would not give our daughters unto the peoples of the land, nor take their daughters for our sons. (10:31)

To resolve to follow the commandments of the *Orit* is the heart of the *Sigd*; and for us how significant is the prohibition against intermarriage, when we are constantly being pushed and pressured to convert and intermingle by "the peoples of the land."

"And yet for all this, we make a sure covenant, and subscribe it ... and our priests set their seal unto it." (10:1)

Second—the *Sigd* is thus a Confirmation of the Covenant made when the Torah was given to Moses on Mount Sinai. Traditionally, the Feast of Weeks is celebrated in the Western World as the time of the Covenant at Sinai and a service of Confirmation is held in many synagogues. This is an affirmation of loyalty to Torah, just like the *Sigd*.

Thus Chapters 19 and 20 of the Book of Exodus are read, telling of Sinai and the Ten Commandments. The sacred works of the Beta Yisrael, *Gadla Abraham* and *Gadla Moses*, telling the stories of the founder and the lawgiver of Beta Yisrael are also read. Perhaps "recited" is a better word than "read" as everything seems to have been committed to memory.

Third—the *Sigd* is a day of fasting, seeking forgiveness and remembering the dead, much in the way of Yom Kippur. In this aspect, the *Sigd* is known by its other name, *mehella* or *mehlella*, which is also the name of observances of the Ethiopian Christian Orthodox Church. As many forms of church worship are based on the Old Testament, it is not surprising that confession, entreaty, *mehilla* ("pardon" in Hebrew) and other features of *Yom Kippur* should be found there too.

Though *Yom Kippur* is observed by the Beta Yisrael as a separate fast day, it has not the central position for them as it has for world Jewry. The result of this is that during these first years in Israel, the Beta Yisrael are in a quandry. It will be some years till Yom Kippur becomes more significant for adults than the *Sigd*. At the same time, being the only ones to celebrate the *Sigd* gives the Beta Yisrael a feeling of being different, while their striving is to show that they are totally a part of the religious community in Israel.

This is just the opposite of the function of the *Sigd* in Ethiopia where it was intentionally a dividing observance which separated the Beta Yisrael from everyone else. There was even a requirement not to touch anyone who was not a Beta Yisrael for a whole week before the Day. Conjugal relations were not allowed for the week either, more stringent than the prohibition at Sinai itself (Exodus 19:15).

There have actually been two *Sigd* observances each year. The split is partly based on the desire of one group to keep to the separatist nature of the holy day. They gather near the U.N. headquarters on a hill across a deep valley with a view of Jerusalem. The other group is integrative in intent and has met on Mount Zion and at the Western Wall. The split may be ending as the continued pain and pressure of families left behind in Ethiopia unites the groups here for concerted action.

As the ban on outside observers has not been applied in Israel, it is hoped that in the future the *Sigd* is to be viewed by a large gathering of Israelis and visitors from overseas as well. An addendum of music and commentary will explain the proceedings in several languages. The *Sigd* itself will remain unchanged, but the message and inspiration of a people that has survived long ages will be shared with the world.

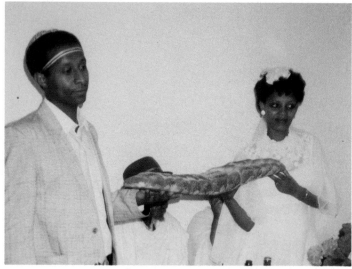

At the *Sigd* on United Nations Hill, Jerusalem, November 1984.

The scene is as it was throughout the ages except for being in Jerusalem... and the microphones.

Formerly, only the *qesoch* prayed and read biblical selections. It is good to have a prayerbook and to follow the chanted words.

The prayers of the women are quieter and perhaps deeper. Their responsibilities are heavy in the new land, and the pain of separation for loved ones is sharper for them.

The place of honor and total respect is given to the elders, so that it is sometimes difficult to distinguish them from the *qesoch*.

In full traditional Ethiopian garb, lovingly guarded and brought to Jerusalem on the long, long trek.

Historic photos of year
when *Sigd* was held on Mount Zion
November 3, 1983

*Their children
also didst Thou multiply
and brought them into this land.*
Nehemiah 9:23

Sigd Remembered

E.A. speaks Hebrew fluently, has completed a commercial course and is highly regarded at work. Her eyes lit up when asked to recount what she could remember of the *Sigd*. Hesitant at first, once she started she couldn't stop remembering.

"I remember going up the hill at Ambover like it was yesterday. We started up at 8 in the morning. It felt like we were going up Mt. Sinai. I mean, there was so much talk about Mt. Sinai and that we were all going to receive the Ten Commandments, it just seemed absolutely real to me as a little girl. I kept looking up to the top to see if Moses was there. Of course, it never occurred to me that he would be anything but a black man.

There were so many people there and all around me. The hill isn't very far away from the village. It is near the public school and maybe about a kilometer more up to the summit. As long as we were below, I could see everything, because it was largely a barren plain, slowly rising to a few small trees. People were coming in long lines from every direction. But once we came close to the crest, it narrowed into a single path and then I could see nothing but mother's back in front of me.

Mother carried an umbrella. We called it *jant'ila*. I think all the ladies did, against the sun. The *jant'ilas* of the *qesoch* were very colorful and special. It seemed they were more than just for shade. There was holiness in them, protecting the *qes*.

Mother also carried quite a large stone on her head all the way up. She walked so gracefully in her white, fringed *qamis*. (She lives in the Galilee now and still has the same beautiful, quiet face and large, unmoving eyes, like a camera ready to take your picture.) Everyone put their stones down in a circle. Even I could put the little one in my hand down, too. Inside the circle the *qesoch* would unwrap the *Orit* and begin the service.

Coming down the hill was the best part. I just wanted to run right down. The sky is such a clean blue then by the end of November and white clouds are already hugging the edge of the hill. I had to control myself a little longer, till the *qesoch* led us all to the *mesgid* and put the *Orit* back in its place.

The fast meant we couldn't drink either. I was just a little girl, but it wasn't hard. Maybe because I knew once we came back down the hill, we would have a big party, with plenty to eat and drink and music and everybody dances. We began celebrating in the afternoon around the *das*, which is a leafy shelter to cover the juicy *wat* and drinks and everything.

Later, our house was jammed with my cousins and everybody. Because they came from far away, they would be sleeping over. I wanted to stay up all night like everybody else. Mother always gave me permission, but that was only because she knew I was so tired I would fall asleep when the sun went down, even before it got dark."

Praying at the *Sigd*, 1983

Prayers at the Sigd

Prayer expressing the longing to re-enact the ancient entry into the Land of Israel—

Here, O Israel to the Law of your G-d... behold you are to cross the Jordan... and he will feed you the manna for forty years as a father feeds his son till you come to the border of Palms (at Jericho where the first crossing was made).

Prayer for loyalty to commandments—

The Torah is close to you... so you can observe it. Behold, I have set before you death and life, the curse and the blessing. Choose!

Prayer to remind people that the tradition is venerable—

May the blessings of the righteous ones be upon you. Our father Abba Sabra was a servant of G-d.
(By tradition, Abba Sabra erected a synagogue in the 15th Century, began the monastic order, and converted the son of King Zara Yaqob to Judaism.)

Translated into Hebrew by Yona Bogale

A page from the *Sigd* prayerbook used in Israel today.

Composite prayer uttered by Ethiopian woman at the *Sigd*, November 1984.

"*Amlaka* Israel ... I haven't forgotten my grandchildren left behind,
I know all of their names, though 3 were born after I left; but they don't know
   me.
I did endless ablutions all of my life to keep myself pure before You.
I cooked for the *qes* and the community for every worship assembly
   for 32 years.
I never violated the Sabbath nor missed a service, except sometimes when ill.
Here, I even put notes in the Wall, "their" way.
Why am I so sorely punished to live without 5 of my children and all my
   grandchildren?"

        As the prayers were making their way up to Heaven, the
news that Operation Moses had begun was making its way
down.

Funeral of *Qes* Uri Ben Baruch in Ashdod—December 23, 1984

יִתְגַּדֵל וְיִתְקַדֵּשׁ...
הוּא יַעֲשֶׂה שָׁלוֹם עָלֵינוּ וְעַל כָּל יִשְׂרָאֵל.
"May He bring Peace upon us... and upon all Israel."

ይትባረክ፡እጊ አብሔር፡አምላከ፡እሥራኤል።

Yitbarak Egzi'abeher Amlaka Israel
"May the Lord, G-d of Israel, be blessed."

The Rabbi and and his father the *qes*.

The *chira* has become a wand of authority in the hand of the *qes*, but it still remains just a flywhisk.

The *qes* is not a rabbi. His functions in Ethiopia included all the duties of a modern rabbi—conducting services, leading prayers, preaching, and teaching—plus some that are not rabbinic functions today, such as ritual preparation of meat and circumcision. Though formally a *Kohen* or priest as described in the Torah, the *qes* also has community duties that parallel today's rabbi—guiding the community and the individual as pastoral advisor. In a way, he is closer to a Chassidic rabbi whose advice is sought after *and followed* in mundane as well as spiritual affairs.

Thus, there is more than the ordinary father and son relationship here. While father and other *qesoch* are always first in opening ceremonials with the ancient prayers, it is the son who is recognized by the State as an official rabbi, presiding over weddings, funerals, and other religious functions where registration and certification is required by Israeli law.

Bridging the gap is the obvious love between the *qes* and all his 10 children who comprise a beautiful family in Israel.

In Ethiopia, the *qes* was spiritual leader of his community, much like the *Rebbe* was to his *Hassidim*. The *qes* walked under his *jant'ila*, the ritual umbrella, and the rabbi walked under his *shtreimel*, the round fur head-dress. These ordinary items became ritual objects of veneration. If the spiritual leader loved and was beloved of his people, the faith found its way around the umbrella or the hat and lodged in the man.

163

After the rally, peace is with the *qesoch* in the glade.

June 14, 1987, in front of the office of the Prime Minister.

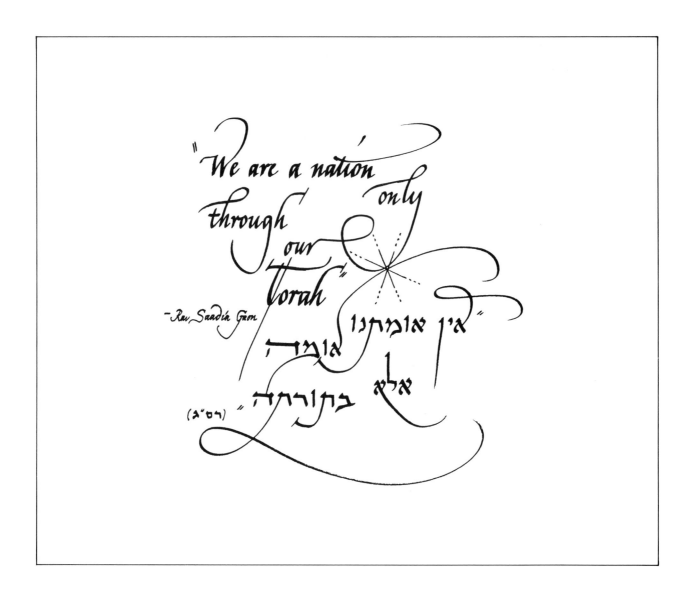

"We are a nation only through our Torah"

—Rav Saadia Gaon

"אין אומתנו אומה אלא בתורה" (רס"ג)

Elders

ሽማግሌ

shimagille

*Wisdom is with the aged
   and understanding (comes)
   with length of days.*

Job 12:2

*The child runs faster,
   but the elder gets there first.*

Ethiopian Proverb

The aged in our day do not fare as well as the verse from Job promises. They are too often pushed into retirement and into quiet corners and allowed to exchange wisdoms with each other.

Beta Yisrael, however, took the matter of age and wisdom quite seriously. The aged were not put out to pasture, but a man's (and sometimes, a woman's) intellectual and spiritual resources were called upon for the guidance of the community. His years alone give him the rank of elder and his grey hair earns respect. If, in addition, he remains clear and persuasive, he will have more than respect—he will be listened to carefully and his counsel sought and followed.

This was an attitude shared by many ancient peoples, notably in the Orient; but, as in most matters, in the case of Beta Yisrael, the direct impetus came from Torah. Three Hebrew words were enough:

Rise up before the aged

Leviticus 19:32

167

Looking up to elders became so fixed a part of the social fabric that it remained intact with the transfer to Israel. No serious family discussions, no major decisions for the community are made until the elders have spoken. And do they speak!

One self-help organization of Ethiopian immigrants in Israel is led by ten vigorous men in their twenties and thirties. Their strength and support comes from an assembly of about one-hundred elders who gather monthly in the synagogue of a Tel Aviv educational institution.

Many come dressed in the same white, home-woven *shemmas* they wore on their backs when they arrived in Israel. Some, wearing *shemmas* obviously improvised from their bedding, seem not reduced thereby in dignity or bearing. One after another they mount the platform or rise in place to express their views—often at great length and always emphatically and with conviction.

The visiting official from a government or voluntary agency is taken aback on his first encounter with an elder in an Amharic speaking milieu. The slim, quiet gentleman who smiles and nods and gets up for you when you enter his room, or is the soul of politeness in your office, barely muttering a Hebrew greeting and tied to his translator—stands here before the assembly, a veritable Demosthenes—better, Isaiah—his personality changed, his speech free flowing and unhesitating, his points obviously well-ordered, emerging with surprising power now that the fetters of language and translators have been removed. His glottalized "ejectives" emphasize his polemic with sonorous explosions that startle you repeatedly and that your palate would be much tested to emulate.

He is among his own. He is a *shimagille* who has recapitulated in his lifetime the history of his people. His years have earned him the right to be heard in honor and the imperative need to share his experience casts upon him the duty of utilizing his full forensic power.

Actually, final decisions on the issues raised—economic, social, educational, religious—will be made by the new generation, but they have heard the opinions of the elders, and they will be influenced by them. Lest anyone think they will disregard or forget what was said, their scribe has been standing on the synagogue platform for hour after hour, holding a large record book in hand, not even leaning it upon a stand, not utilizing a tape recorder, but following the old way and writing summary minutes of the noble words.

The late afternoon sun sends a reddish glow into the spacious synagogue. Many hours of debate have passed, and now some wander into the yard. A bit of water is taken, a bit of food is quietly unwrapped from a bag or paper fold. The elders have had many years of practice in abstinence from many things, too often including food.

As the elder speaks—at meetings, such as the one described; at public gatherings or demonstrations for the promotion of the cause; at local meetings in crowded living rooms at absorption centers where the issue may be whether to pressure for a move to separate, private apartments, or to acquiesce and try to upgrade the quality of life under existing conditions; at all occasions where thought and passion must be wrapped in words—the discourses of the wise one are tinged, often explicitly, with an element his forebears knew not. It is an element of wonder and humility that he is not speaking back in the village, surrounded by unfriendly neighbors and enveloped by a threatening future. Somehow, because of the merits of his fathers, he was privileged to reach the land of promise, the land of Jerusalem.

A mixture of sadness and anger, unworthiness and faith, envelopes him as he realizes the difference between the aged here and the aged there in these fateful years of the waning twentieth century.

Here, the elderly are the smallest part of the immigrant population. There, the percentage is very high. They were left behind *because* they were old and most couldn't make the journey.

Here, they have a large measure of tranquility and a traditional role to play out among their loved ones. There, they face a nightmare of uncertainty. A two-edged sword hangs over their heads—intolerable conditions and an intolerable separation from their children and grandchildren in Israel. Jerusalem still remains a dream, a place to long for, the goal and repository of endless prayers.

Here, even the *shimagille* wonders if he should really put a note into a crack in the Western Wall. The crack is already overstuffed with notes. Besides, he doesn't really write that well. Anyway, won't *egzi'abeher* be confused to find a prayer in Ge'ez in this place?

There, the wise one wonders what has happened to the thousands of prayers his forefathers have been sending to Jerusalem for two and a half thousand years. Is there room for all of them? Will there be room for his? In the end, he has no doubt that his prayers will arrive—that someone is listening.

How close the Beta Yisrael would have felt to the Jews of the world, had they realized that for all the centuries since the destruction of Jerusalem and the second Temple, world Jewry was scattered everywhere in an exile of its own, often harsh and bitter. Thrice daily the dispersed prayed: "May our eyes see Thy return to Zion." The *qes* uttered similar words more often.

A Hebrew poem by Avigdor Hameiri, set as a stirring song, expresses the prayers of the Jews of the world returned to Jerusalem.

Though not so intended, it speaks as well for the House of Israel returned to Zion from Wollo and Tigre, Wolqayt, Gondar, and the Mountains of Simien.

> *Greetings of peace, O Jerusalem,*
> *From the top of Mount Scopus I send.*
>
> *Generations one hundred I've dreamed of you*
> *With you our sorrows would end.*
>
> *Be blessed, be blessed, O city of kings.*
> *He comes, the Messiah, the exiles he brings!*

Friendship

Reading a Newsletter published in Amharic—or looking at the pictures.

With the basic letters and variants forming an alphabet of 256 letters, it is little wonder that farmers had no time to learn to read or write the language they speak so beautifully. And who had schools?

In Israel, they have come into a Golden Age of leisure and learning. Now the elders can read Hebrew—a language they don't understand... and still can't read Amharic, a language they do.

Solution: An Amharic-Hebrew dictionary has been prepared, listing Amharic words written also in transliteration with Hebrew letters. Result: Illiterate no longer!

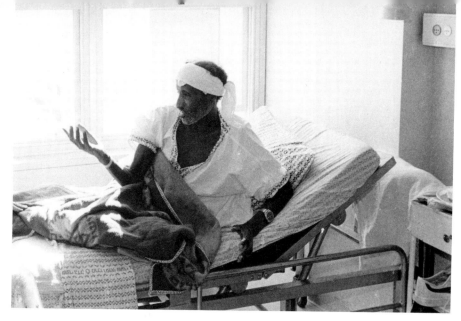

From infants to the elderly, there was excellent, and usually quick response of Beta Yisrael to treatment of a host of diseases they came with.

Thanks to modern medicine, says the hospital...

And to plenty of injections, say the Beta Israel, strong believers in the magic of the needle...

And to *egzi'abeher* (G-d), add the elderly with reverence.

The New Year of Trees is not in the Torah and thus was not a festival on the Beta Yisrael calendar.

But it's pleasant enough. Eat some Israel grown fruits and nuts, sing some songs, plant a tree. Lovely.

This tall, beautiful woman almost fills her small apartment in the Carmiel Absorption Center with her large frame.

"I came alone, for I could walk. But my husband was too old to walk. He was not well, and I was sure I would never see him again. They made me come, he made me come, the children made me come. I didn't want to, but I came."

"Then," she cries as she recalls it, "after two years of waiting, good people helped us... and suddenly, he was here! How? In a plane, in a plane!"

Beta Yisrael elders possess time, dignity and authority; and they go out among the multitude to inspire and search for justice for the forgotten remnant of their people.

I applied my heart to seek and to search out by wisdom concerning all things that are done under heaven...

Ecclesiastes 1:13

I returned, and saw under the sun, that the race is not to the swift, nor the battle to the strong... but time and chance happened to them all.

Ecclesiastes 9:11

Hazkara—Spring 1985

First Annual Memorial Day for the thousands who died in Ethiopia or perished on the secret roads to Jerusalem. Trees were planted this day to keep their spirit and the meaning of their sacrifice alive.

"How was it all etched so deeply into my eyes?"

A respected elder, concerned about his family left behind, desperately searches for ways to save them.

Another moving face—the three head coverings on this page are a paradigm of acculturation.

Class break at the Gilo Absorption Center, Jerusalem.

For many men this age, it's not *back* to school, it's the first time they've ever been in a formal classroom.

Rabbi Yose said: Whoever honors the Torah will himself be honored by men...
Ethics of The Fathers 4:8

רבי יוסי אוֹמֵר: כל הַמְכַבֵּד אֶת הַתּוֹרָה,
גּוּפוֹ מְכֻבָּד עַל הַבְּרִיּוֹת

At Holy Day of the *Sigd*, 1983

A man's wisdom makes his face to shine.
Ecclesiastes 8:1

Yaakov and Rivka
A Couple of Distinction

Back in Ethiopia, Yaakov was a man of means with a reputation for generosity and ability. For 27 years, he regularly donated the turbans, *matamtamiya*, for all the *qesoch* plus pencils, pens, and exercise books for all the children from first to sixth grade in the Ambover Jewish schools. He was also a noted healer with special talents and insights with which he was able to cure many in body and soul. People sought him out for advice and arbitration.

Most of his possessions were taken away from him in the social and political upheavals that racked Ethiopia but he retained some land and cattle and was the only *awaqi* (healer, wise man) who was allowed by the authorities to continue in his profession.

During the 1967 Six Day War, Yaakov slept on the floor and prayed earnestly for Israel. He made a vow to give thirty Ethiopian *birr* (dollars) to the Holy Temple in Jerusalem and put this money under his bed. Early in 1986, he and his wife Rivka—his faithful partner in all his endeavors for forty years—left all their remaining possessions and joyfully came to Israel. Upon landing at Lod, Yaakov took out those 30 Ethiopian dollars and asked to whom he could give them. They were finally donated to a Soldiers' Fund.

At last—this gracious couple fulfilled their dream of a lifetime—and the dream of their forefathers—when together with their children they could walk in Jerusalem and establish a new home in the Land of Israel.

The venerable face inspired confidence… and when the eyes and mouth speak, their wisdom was apparent.

Woman of Valor

Chapter 31 of Proverbs describes the Jewish Woman of distinction.

> *She looketh well to the ways of her household,*
> *And eateth not the bread of idleness.*
> *Her children rise up and call her blessed;*
> *Her husband also, and he praiseth her.*

These qualities of hard work, total devotion to her husband and children and to her G-d, describe the *wayzaro*, the Ethiopian woman of achievement quite as well:

> *She opens her hand to the needy... She is robed in strength*
> *and dignity and fears not the final day.*

The tradition of honoring the Woman of Valor is not forgotten in Israel today as illustrated by the following events...

By eight in the morning, the home was filled with guests... among them 7 or 8 distinguished *qesoch*, the spiritual leaders of the Ethiopian Jewish community, gathered for the *tazkar* memorial service. Dressed in white, their heads crowned with the *matamtamiya* (turban), the priests were generally distinguishable among the crush of people around the coffee table in the small living room. Some of the other men were also dressed in the white *shemma*, but it was their prayers and their lengthy eulogies and amens that identified the *kahenat* (kohanim). The prayers and amens were moving and evocative even to the Western ear.

The congestion and activity was even greater in the small kitchen. Washed and cleaned lamb was being sliced into a huge mound to become *yebeg wat*, a succulent spicy stew. *Injera*, flat breads, were being baked under conditions much more difficult than the open fires and fields "back home" in the Ethiopian hill country around Lake Tana. Slightly built women were lugging in cases of beer and cola brought up to the fifth floor from the market downstairs. The beer wasn't the same as the home fermented *t'ella*, but one has to make do. There would be plenty to eat and drink for all who came, and many were expected.

"Isn't all this very expensive?" a guest inquired discreetly. The answer came in a whisper.

The handmade baskets are lovely in Israel, too.

"We are all like one family here. And especially for such an honored woman, everyone wants to help."

The "honored woman" was known simply as Zawoditu. We assumed that news of her recent death had just reached Israel, bringing about this memorial service. It turned out that she had actually died three years ago waiting for the airlift to the Promised Land. Zawoditu was one of those who did not make it, the whisperer explained. "She died *al kiddush Hashem*, sanctifying the Name. Surely we can say that of every Ethiopian Jew who gave up life itself trying to reach Jerusalem."

Zawditu honored the Name in ways other than through her death. She is spoken of in reverent tones as a sainted woman widely known for her wisdom and kindness. The integrity and staying power of Ethiopian Jewry is confirmed in this reenactment in Israel of a memorial service in the full tradition of this ancient people. That a woman in her own right and based on her deeds and piety was renowned throughout the Jewish villages is itself a testimonial to the values of this amazing people.

"But why," the guest asked, "did you wait so long to hold this service?"

"Because we wanted to move out of the absorption center first, and to feel we are settled in our own place. Today we are kind of bringing our dear mother home to us. Now we ask the people of Israel to bring our living relatives home to us, too. Only then will we know that we are really here."

Making *injera* in an Israeli kitchen.

Yona Bogale
The Man and His Time
1911 — 1987

Yona Bogale followed in the footsteps of his teacher, Jacques Faitlovitch, and expended all his efforts to bettering the lot of the Beta Yisrael. He, too, strove to free them from a cruel bondage and yearned to lead them to the Land of Israel. In this they were both like Moses; but it is Yona's tall and inspiring figure that conjures up the image of Moses more readily.

"Now the man Moses was very meek" the Torah says in Numbers 12:3. (Two verses earlier, we are told he married an Ethiopian woman and G-d, Himself, supports him in this when Miriam and Aaron chide him.) It was this contrasting quality of meekness in a strong and determined leader that characterized Yona.

Those who came to know and love him in his later years in Israel testified to this quality, as did those who were able to recall his oft heroic efforts in Ethiopia. A 1970 photo in David Kessler's *The Falashas* shows Yona with the young settlers he inspired to clear and cultivate bush land near the Sudanese border.

Standing naturally with the toiling workers, Yona seems to be merely part of the scene in this casual snapshot; but his hands in his pockets have the force of Moses' arms held aloft in battle. This was a battle too, as 100 young Ethiopians struggled for five years, and were succeeding in growing and marketing a number of crops. This was one of a succession of efforts organized by Yona to gain a measure of economic independence for his people, and it ended only when the revolution came to power.

● *December, 1983.* A minister, members of the Knesset and leaders of the country have gathered to debate what to do about the Ethiopian Jews. Impassioned speeches are made. The fate of his people is being debated, yet Yona, at 73, sits quietly along the wall. His burning eyes are a challenge. He doesn't speak, but the assembled can't ignore him. The minister says "Yona Bogale is here. We must give answer to his lifetime of striving."

All of his life, Yona followed the teaching of Rabbi Hillel as written in the book he had come to love as a young boy:

> *Be of the disciples of Aaron—love peace and pursue peace, love*
> *people and bring them near to Torah.*
>
> The Ethics of The Fathers 1:12

● *November, 1984.* The photograph shows Yona at the *Sigd* on a hill. He looks down at Jerusalem, a picture postcard in the distance. He answers a question:

"The *Sigd* means longing for Jerusalem, so naturally, it meant more to us there, when we were far away and couldn't reach it. This is the earthly Jerusalem. I suppose we were really longing for the heavenly one."

Yona Bogale

• *1985—After Operation Moses.* Yona is honored at the Knesset as the man who kept his people's hope alive during hopeless years. The years went like this: Born in Wolleka in 1910. Faitlovitch takes him in hand. Hebrew studies in Addis Abeba. At 13 to Jerusalem. At 15 to Frankfurt-Main, at 19 to Switzerland, then to Paris... all Jewish schools. At 21 back to Addis to teach Jewish children.

• *1936—The Italian Invasion.* Anti-Jewish feeling is fostered. Yona is on the move from village to village and manages to survive till Haile Selassie returns to power. Yona is awarded a post in the Ministry of Finance, then Education. He is persuaded to direct the new Jewish school in Asmara, though his leaving the Ministry displeases the Emperor. He is suspected also of actively helping people get to Israel.

What can he do? Can he neglect Jewish children and the Land of Israel to please the Lion of Judah?

Israeli experts come to advise and work in Ethiopia, and in 1953 Yona begins sending students to Kfar Batya, who will then return to teach. The Emperor wants them to utilize the agricultural skills they have learned. Yona promotes this, and still manages to establish schools in eight villages with hundreds of students.

> *He who increases Torah, increases life;*
> *He who increases schooling, increases wisdom;*
> *He who acquires a good name, it is his to keep...*
>
> Ethics of The Fathers 2:8

Crises are endless in his life: the split with the community in Tigre Province; the drastic reduction of money for Jewish schools from Israel; the struggle for the right to come to Israel under the Law of Return. The Emperor breaks relations with Israel because of the Yom Kippur War, and in 1974 is himself deposed and dies.

Through all this a small migration to Israel has continued, and by 1979 there are about 300 Beta Yisrael in Israel with some of Yona's sons amongs them. That year many Beta Yisrael fled to Sudan to escape increased repression. The American Association for Ethiopian Jews assists Yona and the rest of his family to reach Israel.

The line of Yona's life and work was clear and unbending. Education of the youth and contact with Israel were essential to keep the hope of the return alive. The students who came back from Israel were faced with the temptations of better posts in Ethiopia where the educated were at a premium. Yona himself could have, at any stage of his life, settled into a comfortable and rewarding post as lecturer in a major European university. Instead, he remained at the side of his people.

Pressures left the scholar little time to write. Still, he produced an Amharic-Hebrew calendar and an Amharic-Hebrew dictionary, both needed to bind ties with Israel. He also wrote an Amharic book, *Yaesra'el baalot hegeggat—Holidays and Feasts of Israel* (Addis Abeba, 1960) describing rabbinic holiday practices. It is based on the *Shulchan Aruch* (Code of Jewish Law) and includes observances previously unknown to Beta Yisrael, such as The Ten Days of Penitence, Hanukkah and Arbor Day. The book ends with numerous selections from *Ethics of The Fathers*, a small, popular work of great insights that could serve as introduction to the world of talmudic teaching.

> *Rabbi Shammai said: Set aside a time for study; say*
> *little and do much, and receive all men with a cheerful*
> *countenance.*
>
> Ethics of The Fathers 1:15

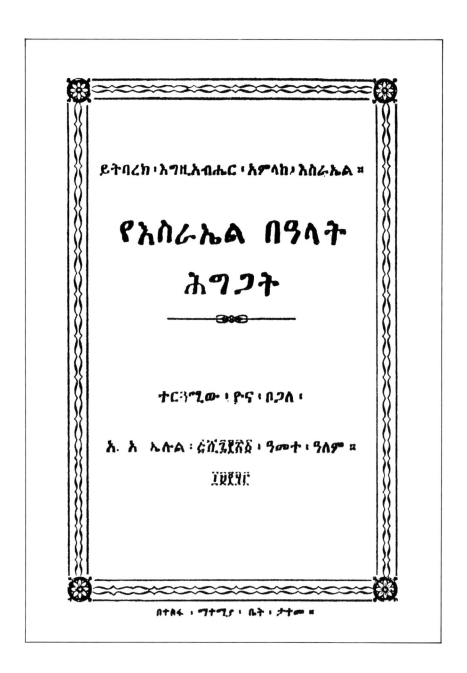

Title page of book written by Yona Bogale called
Holidays and Feasts of Israel

● *August 16, 1987*. Shlomo Hillel, the Speaker of the Knesset, many Israeli rabbis and dignitaries and the largest gathering of Ethiopian Jews in the history of Israel met at the Givat Shaul Cemetery in the hills of Jerusalem. The columns of people, ten abreast, moved wave after wave through the broad paths of the cemetery. The endless line was estimated at over 4,000. That means more than half of all the adult community of Beta Yisrael that had come home to Israel accompanied Yona Bogale to his final resting place in the hills of Jerusalem.

זכר צדיק לברכה

The memory of a righteous man is a blessing forever.

Proverbs 10:7

Ten things were created Sabbath eve at the twilight hour (on the 6th day, after all the world and man and woman were created, G-d, Himself added a few things that no one else could make.) Among them

The Rainbow, sign of the Promise...
The Rod of Moses...
The Tablets of the Ten Commandments...
The Grave of Moses.

Ethics of The Fathers 5:9

The grave of Moses had to be accounted for, because of Deuteronomy 34:6— *And He buried Him... and no one knows where to this day.* G-d buried him, say the rabbis, in that grave He had prepared for him at creation. The intent of the unknown tomb is that not a sepulchre, but his deeds and teachings become the monument of Moses.

So will it be with Yona Bogale, the leader and teacher whose life was a bridge between Ethiopia and Israel. When he was acclaimed in the Knesset, he accepted the recognition on behalf of his courageous people, and he said:

"We are grateful beyond words to the Government of Israel and to those who gave us succor, for the great act of rescue you have performed.

One could say truly that you have brought the 'dry bones out of their grave.' Those who have come are beginning to acquire 'flesh and sinews' and to become human again. For us, the Messiah has already come. We did not expect him so soon; but if we are here in Israel, he has surely come.

There are still many, however, whom he has not yet redeemed, who are suffering the same hunger and insecurity... and we still do not know what will become of them..."

"A good name is better than precious oil."
(Ecclesiastes 7:1)

הצילו יהודים מאתיופיה
SAVE ETHIOPIAN JEWRY

אזור
מוגדל

SELECTED BIBLIOGRAPHY

Baron, Salo W. *A Social and Religious History of the Jews*. New York: Columbia University Press, 1983.

Gruber, Ruth. *Rescue—The Exodus of the Ethiopian Jews*. New York: Atheneum. 1987.

Hancock, G. *The Challenge of Hunger*. London: Victor Gallanz, 1985.

Kessler, David. *The Falashas*. New York: Schocken Books, 1985.

Leslau, Wolf. *Falasha Anthology — The Black Jews of Ethiopia*. New Haven: Yale University Press, 1951.

Messing, Simon D. *The Story of the Falashas*. New York: Balshon Printing Co., 1982.

National Geographic, Vol. 163, No. 5, May 1983, "Ethiopia." Article and photographs by Robert Caputo.

Parfitt, Tudor. *Operation Moses*. London: Weidenfeld and Nicholson, 1985.

Rapoport, Louis, *The Lost Jews*. New York: Stein and Day, 1980.

Rapoport, Louis. *Redemption Song*. New York: Harcourt Brace Jovanovich, 1986.

Safran, Claire. *The Secret Exodus: The Story of Operation Moses*. New York: Prentice Hall Press, 1987.

Shmuel, Abraham, with Arlene Kushner. *Treacherous Journey*. New York: Shapolsky Publishing, 1985.

The Jews of Ethiopia — A People in Transition. Tel Aviv: The Nahum Goldman Museum of the Diaspora, 1986 (Photos and Essays). Editorial Committee: Y. Avner, N. Berger, K.K. Shelemay, U. Ram. Essays by: S. Kaplan, I. Grinfeld, K.K. Shelemay, C. Rosen.

Waldman, Menachem. *The Jews of Ethiopia — The Beta Israel Community*. Jerusalem: Ami-Shav, 1985 (illustrated).

Wurmbrand, Max. *The Falashas*. Encyclopedia Judaica. Jerusalem: Keter, 1971.

Novels

Farhi, Moris. *The Last of Days*. New York: Crown, 1983.

Levitin, Sonia. *The Return*. New York: Artheneum, 1987.

Other Sources Consulted or Quoted

Abbink, Jan. *Segd Celebration in Ethiopia and Israel*. West Germany: Anthropos, International Review of Ethnology and Linguistics, 1983, pp. 789-810.

Aescoly, A.Z. *The Book of the Falashas*, Second edition. Jerusalem: Reuben Mass Press, 1973 (Hebrew).

Alpert, Hava. *History and Customs of Ethiopian Jews*. Jerusalem: American Association for Ethiopian Jews, 1958 (Hebrew).

Gordon, Uri. *Jerusalem Post* Magazine, April 17, 1987 (Quoted on p. 63).

Halévy, Joseph, *Prieres des Falashas*. Paris: 1877.

Halévy, Joseph. *Travels in Abyssinia*. London: 1877.

Kahana, Yael. *Life Among Our Black Brothers*. Tel Aviv: 1977 (Hebrew).

Leslau, Charlotte and Wolf. *African Poems and Love Songs*. Mount Vernon, N.Y.: Peter Pauper Press, 1970.

Leslau, Charlotte and Wolf. *African Proverbs*. New York: The Peter Pauper Press, 1982. (Source of some Ethiopian Proverbs quoted in text.)

Leslau, Wolf. "A Falasha Book of Jewish Festivals," in *For Max Weinreich*, pp. 183-191. London: Mouton & Co., 1964.

Passow, Meyer. *Exotic and Vanished Jewish Tribes*. Tel Aviv: Women's International Zionist Organization (WIZO), 1973.

Rosen, Dr. Chaim. Series of Monographs on Ethiopian Jews. Jerusalem: Hadassah Council in Israel, 1986-1988.

Sahle, Selassie. *Shinega's Village*. Translated from Chaha by Wolf Leslau, Berkeley: University of California Press, 1964.

The Day of Segd. Tel Aviv: National Council for Ethiopian Jews, 1984.

The Seventh Candle, conceived and written by Yosef Miller, 1986.

Wurmbrand, Max. *Arde'et—The Falasha Book of the Disciples*. Tel Aviv: 1963.

R. Yitzchak, Z. Yanir and H. Polani, editors. *Stories by Ethiopian Jews*. Jerusalem: Ministry of Education and Culture, 1986 (Hebrew).

"Tale of the Goat and the Leopard", told by Dani Asmani.

"Money from Heaven" (called "The Lazy Husband"), told in Amharic by Nachum Ayeli.

AMHARIC GLOSSARY

Amharic is the national language of Ethiopia. The word (Hebrew), following a definition means there is a similar word in the Hebrew language. Many of the Amharic words have their origin in Ge'ez. Some of the words listed here are not in the text but are included for their interest.

abbat — father
ababa — flower
amlaka — King of the Universe (G-d)
amole ch'aw — bar of coarse salt
ankelba — pouch used to carry baby on back
arfe asart — monthly festival
astasreyo — Day of Atonement (*Yom Kippur*)
ato — mister
awaqi — wise man
balabbat — homeowner (Hebrew)
barakete — festive bread, blessed (Hebrew)
berhan sarraka — New Year Festival (*Rosh Hashana*)
beta sab — family
beta yisrael — House of Israel (Hebrew)
birr — Ethiopian dollar
buda — to be of evil-eye, satanic
bunna — coffee
cheqla — young child
ch'ira — flywhisk
cush — Biblical term for Ethiopia
dabbo — Sabbath bread
dabtara — learned, religious functionary
das — leafy hut
dawit — Psalms of David (Hebrew)
dergue — Marxist revolutionary committee
dulla — stick
elell elell — cry of joy
elohe — G-d (Hebrew)
endod — soapwart plant for washing clothes
eskesta — shoulder dance
falasha — stranger, invader, exile (historical name, presently considered derogatory)
fasika — Passover (*Pesach*, Hebrew)
fech — divorce
ge'ez — ancient sacred language of Ethiopia
gelulat — ceramic crown on synagogues
gezrat — circumcision
hesan — infant
injera — flat, round, spongy daily bread
innat — mother
jabana — coffee pot
jant'ila — ritual umbrella
kahen — priest (*Kohen*, Hebrew)
kahenat — priesthood, priests
kayla — once a blacksmith, now an insult
kebra negast — *Glory of Kings*, Ethiopian national epic
keshera — tying of headbands at wedding (Hebrew)
krar — stringed lyre
lijinnet — childhood

mamcha — rod to strike cymbal at prayer
manokse — monk
maqdas — shrine
ma'rar — Harvest Festival (*Shavuot* in Hebrew)
margam bet — the menstrual hut
masob — basket
matamtamiya — white turban of *qes*
mender — village
mesgid — synagogue (Muslim source)
nagarit — drum
neber — leopard
negus — king
orit — Beta Yisrael Bible
qachel — metal gong for prayer rhythms
qamis — a dress
qedesta-qdussan — Holy of Holies (Hebrew)
qes — rabbi/priest, same as *kahen*
qesoch — plural of *qes*
qita — unleavened bread (*matza* in Hebrew)
qurban — sacrifice (Hebrew)
rufael — Raphael, healing angel (Hebrew)
salot — prayer
salota bet — prayer house, synagogue
sanbat — Sabbath (*Shabbat*, Hebrew)
sanbat salam — Sabbath peace (greeting, Hebrew)
sansel — hand-held rattle or sistrum
seyon — Zion, the holy ark (Hebrew)
shamye — necklace
shemma — wrap-around, white toga
shifta — bandit, professional robber
shimagille — elder, wise person
shum — government officer
sigd — Holy day of Repentance and longing
som — fast day (Hebrew)
tabot — Holy Ark (Hebrew)
tajj — honey made drink
tazkar — memorial service (*Hazkara* in Hebrew)
t'ella — barley beer
tef — grain (like barley), grown only in Ethiopia
tena-adam — herbal air filter for nostril
t'ena yest'elen — Hello, good-bye
tukul — hut (Ethiopian village home)
wat or *wot* — spiced sauce stew. Dip for *injera*
wayzaro — respected lady, Mrs.
ya'aras gojo — maternity shelter
yitbarak — may He be blessed (Hebrew)
zamad — blood relative, close friend
zar — spirit

MEET AND GREET!

Amharic Greetings and Phrases

These phrases may be useful whether you travel to Ethiopia or meet the Beta Yisrael who are everywhere in Israel. Speaking a word or two at least shows your interest, that you cared enough to learn to ask "How are you?" Watch the faces light up with surprise and pleasure when you approach and say "endemin allu?"

Phrase	Transliteration (Anglicized)
Greetings	t'ena yest'elen
Good morning	endemin adderu
Good day	dehna walu
Good evening	endemin ameshu
Goodbye	dehna hunu
How are you?	endemin allu?
My name is —	sime... nagn
What is your name?	man yibalallu?
Tell me your story	tarikwon yingerugn
Welcome	enquan dehna mettu
Let us have coffee	bunna innitetta
Please help me	esti aggizegn ibakewo
I would like to help you	ene ananten lemerdat efellgallehu
Please	ebakwo
Thank you	amasginallahu
Excuse me	yikirta
Never mind (it is nothing)	gid yellam
Yes	awo
No	yellem
All right	eshi
This	yihe
It is good	tiru no
It is not good	tiru aydellem
I am sorry	aznallehu
I cannot	alchilim
I feel hot	muket yissemagnal
Cold	bird
Aspirin	aspro
Take me to	wode... yiwsedugn
Where is the market?	gebeya yet no?
Which direction?	beyet bekkul no?
Where is the?	yet no?
Where do you come from?	keyet mettu?
What do you want?	min yifelligallu?
Where are you going?	wodet yihedallu?
Where is the restroom?	shint beit yet no?
Where is the telephone?	telephone yet no?
A glass of water, please	wuha yisettugn
Do you have a pencil?	ersas allewo?
How much is this?	sint no?
Where?	yet?
When?	metche?
Why?	lemin?
How?	endet?
It is beautiful work	asdennaki sira no
The food was delicious	mighibu tafach nebbere
Your dress is beautiful	libswo yamral
Good Sabbath	sanbat salam
Thank G-d	Egziabher yimesghen

PHOTOGRAPHER CREDITS

Numbers refer to text pages on which their photographs appear.
L=Left side, R=Right side.

Zev Ackerman, Jerusalem
30, 38 lower, 52 lower L, 53, 57 upper L, 58, 60, 67 lower, 80, 102 center, 103, 117, 118, 126, 144, 188.

Colette Berman, Jerusalem/Los Angeles
34 upper R, center L, lower L, 39 lower R, 43, 52 upper R and center, 54 L, 55, 57 lower R, 59 corners, 61 lower, L, 82 upper L and lower R, 83, 86 upper and center, 87, 88, 91 center, 98 upper R and lower L, 102 upper L, upper center, upper R, lower center, 107, 109, 121 upper, 123 upper, 124 lower R, 125 upper and lower, 127, 128, 147 lower, 148, 163 lower, 167, 178 center, 181, 194, 195.

Debbi Cooper, Jerusalem
9, 27, 32 lower, 40, 49, 50, 62, 64 upper, 67 upper, 68 upper, 70, 84, 143 upper, 161, 175, 184, 186, 187.

Shmuel Itemnun, Jerusalem
102 lower L, 154 R.

Tzachi Litov, Jerusalem
73, 165, 182, 183

Joe Malcolm, Jerusalem
52 lower R, 81 lower, 98 upper L, 101, 102 lower R, 106, 124 upper R and L, 131, 154 lower, 172, 180 lower, 185.

Sandu Mandrea, Jerusalem
56, 59 center, 92, 120 upper, 142, 164.

Margo Miller, Chicago
119.

Yosef Miller, Netanya
34 upper L, center R, lower R, 35 lower, 39 upper, 41, 51, 52 upper L, 54 upper and lower, 57 lower L, 61 upper, 64 lower, 65, 86 lower, 88, 89, 91 upper and lower, 93, 94, 95 center, 96, 97, 100 lower, 104, 121 R, 122 upper L, lower L and R, 123 lower, 125 L, 129, 143 lower, 145, 147 upper, 149, 155, 156, 163 upper, 173, 174 lower, 178 upper and lower, 190, 194, 195.

Malka Shani, Givatayim
32 upper, 35 upper, 38 upper L and R, 57 upper R, 63, 68 lower, 69, 82 upper R, lower L.

Israel Talby, Hadera
Front and back Jacket, 26, 36, 37, 61 lower R, 72, 77, 78, 100 upper, 105, 120 lower, 122 upper R, 133, 153, 154 upper L, 171, 194, 195.

Israel Defense Forces - Spokesman, Tel Aviv
99 lower L.

Israel Government Press Office, Jerusalem
2, 3, 31, 47, 48, 71, 79, 81 upper, 90, 130, 157, 159, 162, 170, 176, 177, 179.

Jewish National Fund Archives, Jerusalem
180 upper.

Shaare Zedek Medical Center, Jerusalem
33.

Shaare Zedek Medical Center/Shlomo Marcus, Jerusalem
23, 28, 29, 174 upper and center.